COUNTERINSURGENCY

WARFARE

JOHN S. PUSTAY, Major, USAF
United States Air Force Academy

Counterinsurgency

Warfare

The Free Press, NEW YORK
Collier-Macmillan Limited, LONDON

Collier-Macmillan Canada, Ltd., Toronto, Ontario

Second Printing May 1966

Library of Congress Catalog Card Number: 65-11319

To

John Jr., Jeanie, Melanie,

Tanya, and Lorraine

Preface

This book is intended to serve as a stepping stone to the formulation of a body of doctrine for counterinsurgency warfare. To develop such a doctrine both for an insurgency-beset developing state and for the United States as the leader of the Free World, it is, of course, first necessary to put the threat of Communist-controlled or Communist-inspired insurgency into proper historical perspective and into the perspectives of the macrocosm—international Cold War—and of the microcosm—the fertile field for insurgency that exists in virtually every underdeveloped nation.

The evolving body of prescriptions for insurgency warfare, as propounded by non-Communist as well as Communist theorists, is then analyzed and tied to the legacy of insurgency warfare as recorded in modern history. The result of this analysis is a model of Communist insurgency warfare in developing areas during the period of strategic nuclear stalemate. This model sets the scene for the analysis of existing methods and tactics designed to counter this threat, for the rejection of methods that have failed or are likely to fail, and for the design of a new body of methodologies in the formulation of a viable counterinsurgency doctrine.

Parameters for the solving of counterinsurgency problems are then presented along with a group of general prescriptions for the employment of military surface and air forces in operations against an insurgency movement at each stage of its development. Appropriate organizational prescriptions are also presented as well as designs for the constructive use—through military-civic action—of indigenous armed forces to counter budding insurgencies and to assist in nation-building endeavors.

A firm distinction is made between operations that should be undertaken by indigenous military and civil forces and those that should be completed by the United States when its forces become involved in assisting a developing state in defeating an insurgency.

This book should be of value to civilian students of the problems of underdevelopment as well as to military students, who must also be schooled in techniques required to quell insurgencies once they evolve into actual warfare between guerrilla forces and the armed forces of the developing state affected.

I am indebted to Josef Korbel, David Bayley, and Charles Micaud for their suggestions on organization. I am especially indebted to B. Vincent Davis, who guided my research and made many valuable suggestions concerning the final organization and presentation of my findings.

I should also like to extend my appreciation to Harold Holtzclaw, Jack Freeman, and Raymond Coble for their proofreading assistance, to Hal Shipps for editorial suggestions, and especially to Arthur T. Hadley, who, despite an exceedingly heavy work load of his own, volunteered his valuable services in editing substantial portions of this work.

I also acknowledge the important contribution made toward the completion of this book by my wife, Lorraine, who—while necessarily burdened by the tasks related to managing our household and rearing our children—nevertheless spent many long hours typing the first two drafts of the manuscript and continually served as a valuable "sounding-board" for ideas which were later translated into action in the preparation of the book in its final form. Finally, I must add a note of appreciation to our young daughters, Tanya, Melanie, and Jeanie, who patiently accepted the "nonavailability" of their father for what, to them, seemed like an awfully long time.

JOHN S. PUSTAY

Contents

Part Two
The Incumbent Regime's Response:
Counterinsurgency Warfare

Part Three
A Proposal for an American Response

COUNTERINSURGENCY

WARFARE

PART ONE

The Theory and Practice
of Communist
Insurgency Warfare

1

Introduction

Forces of change will profoundly alter the international order within the next decade. This is a difficult factor to be considered in national security planning. The most drastic change will take place in the developing nations. In this drama of transmutation, there will be three principal actor groups: the West, the Communist East, and the underdeveloped states. The use of the term *Communist East* or *Communist bloc*, as we will see later, does not imply a monolithic political-ideological entity.

It is safe to assume that the fundamental incompatibility between the ideologies of the West and the Communist East will tend mutually to invite conflict or, at the very minimum, active competition between member states of these two blocs. The advent of thermonuclear warheads and of sophisticated delivery vehicles has, however, placed tremendous restraints on the modes of such conflict. The very nature of the politico-military alliance systems among the technologically advanced members of these two opposing camps (that is, the North Atlantic Treaty Organization and the Warsaw Pact) tends to minimize the probability that the related areas will be military battlefields.

In contrast, the situation in the underdeveloped areas is conducive to their becoming the battleground for such con-

flict. In the first place, the general political situation within
these nations, whether or not they are committed by alliance
to either camp, is somewhat blurred. This blurring is a reflection of domestic sociopolitical instability, a by-product of their
quest for modernity. Such situations appear to be most pronounced in those states that are either uncommitted or allied
to the West and are attempting their modernization under a
canopy of political freedom. Here indigenous Communist
parties actively catalyze existing instability and attempt to dis-
lodge committed states from the Western camp, or bring the
uncommitted into the Communist camp as either full members or at least sympathetic fellow travelers.

Given the prescriptions of Communist ideology, the nature
of modern thermonuclear war, and the unstable and exploitable nature of the developing states, it appears that the modes
of conflict between the West and the Communist states will
probably be indirect, muted, and somewhat ambiguous. It is
equally apparent that this conflict will be centered in the
underdeveloped areas.

In view of this situation and the lessons of recent history—
the 1962 India-China military conflict notwithstanding—the
future actions of the USSR and, to a somewhat lesser degree,
Communist China, become rather obvious. In pursuing their
international goals, these Communist-camp leadership states
will supplement conventional diplomacy and economic aid
with subversive, unconventional, and unacknowledged offensive politico-military operations. The principal "vehicle" for
these operations will most likely be insurgency warfare. The
veneer of their innocence in these wars will be transparently
thin; it will be specifically designed to delay, blunt, or even
forestall Western interference or retribution.

It is essential at this point to define *insurgency warfare*.
Unfortunately, there is little consensus even among the experts
as to just what the term means. Such phrases as "unconventional warfare," "irregular warfare," "internal war," "guerrilla
war," "insurgency," "insurrection," "rebellion," "revolution,"

and "people's liberation war" undoubtedly present the lay reader—and perhaps even some experts—with a formidable array of like-meaning terms. One is then forced either to dismiss these terms as jargon—"all the words mean the same thing"—or to accept them and meticulously distinguish between each term. This adds confusion to a general subject which is already complex by its nature. In discussing this problem, Professor Samuel P. Huntington remarked, somewhat facetiously, "No doubt each term serves some purpose, although one cannot help but feel that semantics has perhaps outstripped theory."[1]

The term *insurgency warfare* as used in this text will refer to that composite conflict phenomenon which can be defined as a cellular development of resistance against an incumbent political regime and which expands from the initial stage of subversion-infiltration through the intermediate stages of overt resistance by small armed bands and insurrection to final fruition in civil war.

Insofar as these stages of insurgency are designed to replace an existing sociopolitical order with a new order which has a different value system, they are revolutionary in character. Insofar as these stages of insurgency are directed against a foreign element, an occupying power, a colonial overseer, they are rebellious. Insofar as the actual clash of arms between insurgents and incumbents is confined to one state, these insurgency stages can be considered as parts of an internal war. Insofar as the insurgent units are small bands employing tactics not conventionally used by regular armed forces, insurgency operations can be described as guerrilla warfare. Finally, insofar as these insurgency stages either are directed by Communists or have an anti-Western orientation, they qualify for Khrushchev's and Kosygin's label of "wars of national liberation."

The path of recent history has been heavily marked by insurgency wars—not all of them successful—in which nations friendly to the United States have become involved. In these

internal wars the indigenous Communist parties, advocating
either social reform or expulsion of the "exploiting imperialists," served as vanguard elements for insurgency. Some examples are the Greek Civil War, the Chinese Civil War, the
Malaya Emergency, the Burmese Civil Wars, the HUK (more
accurately, the HMB, Hukbong Magpalaya Nang Bayan—
People's Liberation Army) rebellion in the Philippines, the
Vietminh, Pathet Lao, and Vietcong insurgencies in Southeast
Asia, and the Castro Revolution in Cuba.[2] However, not all
insurgency wars within the Western and uncommitted areas
during this period were Communist dominated or even motivated. The Indonesian, Moroccan, Tunisian, and Algerian
revolutions are cases in point. Nevertheless, the number of
Communist-sponsored, Communist-captured, and Communist-
controlled insurgency operations is significant and is indica-
tive of the Communist adoption of this mode of conflict for
offensive actions in the international arena. Continued success
in similar endeavors over a long period of time can so weaken
the West that these states could claim total victory via extended series of insurgencies with a minimum expenditure of
their own resources.

It is obviously imperative that the United States, and the
West in general, design and employ appropriate doctrine and
instrumentalities to aid in the prevention of insurgency warfare in the developing areas. Because such action will be too
late for some nations, it is equally obligatory that similar steps
be taken to facilitate and orient American assistance to states
already directly involved in combating this Communist operation.

The logical prerequisite for the formulation of effective
counterinsurgency doctrine and for the creation of efficient
instrumentalities both for preventive and therapeutic operation is, of course, a proper understanding of the phenomenon
of insurgency warfare itself. This is the aim of Part One of
this book. Chapter 2 attempts to place this phenomenon in its
proper Cold War perspective by describing both its internal

(domestic) and external (international) dimensions and their interrelationships. Chapter 3 considers insurgency warfare in its historical perspective. It surveys and analyzes the theory of this warfare with heavy emphasis on the various mutations that have occurred since this theory was given its most significant expression in the 1930's in the writings of Mao Tse-tung. Chapter 4 contains a model of Communist insurgency warfare in the thermonuclear space era. This construct is an attempt at an original synthesis of the theoretical prescriptions of Communist doctrine on insurgency warfare as they have evolved during the middle period of this century with the official historical record of Communist insurgency warfare in the post-World War II period.

The second part of this book is devoted to the formulation and analysis of doctrinal prescriptions designed to counter this Communist threat in the emerging nations of Asia, Latin America, and Africa.

Before turning to Chapter 2, a few explanatory comments are necessary. Occasionally we shall use illustrations of a particular tactic or strategic concept from the non-Communist insurgencies that have taken place in underdeveloped areas since 1945 (and also from Communist-directed insurgencies in Nazi-occupied Europe during World War II). This apparent inconsistency is necessary because in some cases the best illustrations of a particular principle of implementation can be found in non-Communist insurgency actions. It is also safe to assume that effective non-Communist refinements of insurgency principles, or innovations thereto, will be adopted by the Communists in their preparations for future revolutions in the emerging states.

A heavy emphasis has been placed on the military aspects of counterinsurgency actions. These military operations are by no means all "destructive" in nature. The indigenous military establishments in the emerging states and the Western military advisers to these nations can accomplish numerous "constructive" operations. Since this constructive mission has not been the object of much research and writing in the past, it will be thoroughly covered in this study. However, it must be appreciated that nation-building and developmental assistance are long-term propositions. Even the short-term programs to alleviate surface grievances will most likely not be evenly and completely applied throughout an affected nation. Therefore, pocket insurgencies will continue to remain a threat.

The very programs designed to promote socioeconomic development (for example, the Alliance for Progress) will in themselves create tensions and dislocations as the old and indigenous way of life is replaced by a new and alien mode of living. Therefore, the military will be called upon to back the civil police in providing stability during this period of social turmoil.

There is yet another consideration. The initiation of insurgency is generally interpreted as a sign that the indigenous Communist leadership believes the incumbent government and its bases of support to be so weak that it cannot effectively meet the challenge of overt military resistance. Initiation of insurgency after the incumbent government has launched a reform program, however, can also signal the beginnings of success for such a program. In other words, the Communist insurgency may be a last-ditch desperation attempt to sow confusion through violence in order to weaken the impact of these reforms upon the general populace. This type of insurgency will most likely occur in many Latin American nations during the "take-off" stages of their Alliance for Progress programs. The stress in this book on the military aspects of counterinsurgency doctrine appears justified.

2

Factors
Contributing to Communist
Insurgency Warfare:
A Cold War Perspective

Insurgency warfare is often thought to be essentially an internal or local political phenomenon. Although this is seldom true even in non-Communist insurgencies, it is certainly not the case in Communist operations which must be framed against the backdrop of the Cold War in the thermonuclear space era.

The occurrence of Communist insurgency warfare in a particular developing state seems to be related to three important factors: conflicting ideology, strategic nuclear stalemate, and internal instability. Although the following analysis tends to suggest this, no attempt is made here to impute causality to these factors. Neither should they be considered as the only relevant elements of the problem. They are, however, the only elements that we are able to isolate at this time. Thus it is important to study them in the hope that our findings will permit future researchers to complete the picture of contributory factors and perhaps find true causative variables.

Conflicting Ideology

This factor has both an external world dimension and an internal local dimension. These dual dimensions imply that the political-ideological gap between Communist insurgents and the incumbents in a particular developing state is not necessarily a direct proportional reflection of the intensity of the Cold War. And there is an important corollary: if there is a significant differential in the world and local gaps as viewed by Moscow or Peiping—or Hanoi for that matter—then the external control over the native insurgents in a developing state will be a function of the degree of dependence of these forces upon the support (both material and diplomatic) of the associated international center of Communism.

A "spirit of Camp David" may prevail in the world as a whole, but an intense Communist insurgency operation may be going on in a particular developing state. Conversely, the Cold War may be raging very hot in the over-all international arena, but a situation within a particular underdeveloped state may dictate an accommodation (probably temporary as viewed by the Moscow-Peiping leadership and the local Communists) between the incumbent government and indigenous Communists. Or, the internal conditions may dictate a maximum effort, but the general cold war situation and the dependence of the insurgents upon the support of Moscow or Peiping may force this insurgent movement to settle for less than total victory. The 1962 settlement of the Communist insurgency war in Laos is such an example. The important point here is that the probability of Communist-initiated insurgency in a given underdeveloped nation can very well be a function both of the international ideological-political gap and concurrently of the local ideological-political gap between the incumbents and insurgents.

Strategic Nuclear Stalemate

This factor is a result of the possession of relatively invulnerable nuclear retaliatory forces by the United States and the USSR and their resolve to use such forces only under conditions of severe provocation. Given this state of affairs and the fact that the ideologies championed by both camps seem mutually to invite conflict, it is obvious that such conflict will not rationally be pursued within the strategic nuclear realm.

The next lower level of conflict, local or limited war, also seems to be foreclosed to the major combatants. There are two reasons for this, if one assumes that the Communist bloc leadership states will continue to be the initiators of offensive actions while the United States resists such actions. First, since the Korean War the United States and the West in general have constructed a respectable nuclear-conventional, limited-war capability. Second, limited war between states of the opposing camps will necessitate that the United States and the USSR become directly involved in order to uphold the integrity of their respective camps. Once these major powers become so involved, the possibilities of escalation—as a result of reciprocal attempts by the two powers to save their prestige in the face of tactical defeat—become great. Hence the possession of a respectable limited-war capability by both West and East and the threat of escalation to strategic nuclear war combine to deter the Communist bloc states from pursuing a West-East conflict at the limited war level.

The level below interstate war on the spectrum of West-East military conflict is insurgency warfare within a particular nation-state. In such wars the Soviet or Chinese Communists can support an insurgency movement either covertly or overtly with material assistance, technical advisers, and even "volunteers." The United States can respond with material, Military Assistance and Advisory Group (MAAG) personnel, Special Forces (guerrilla-trained regular troops), and helicopter forces with air and ground crews included. The commitment of prestige by the East or West leadership states in their involvement in these types of internal war is significantly less than that related to assistance in interstate limited wars. Thus the problem of escalation is considerably reduced.

The Soviet View—In Khrushchev's now-famous January 6, 1961, speech, in which he reported to selected high party organs on the just-concluded conference of Communist parties of 81 nations, the Soviet Premier clearly indicated his full appreciation of the extant East-West situation of strategic mutual deterrence:

> Comrades, questions of war and peace were at the center of attention at the conference. The participants were fully aware that the problem of preventing a global thermonuclear war is the most burning and vital problem for mankind. . . . There is no more urgent task than the prevention of such a catastrophe. . . .
>
> Communists are the most determined opponents of world wars, just as they are generally *opponents of wars among states*.[1] (Italics added.)

Turning to the subject of "limited" or "local" wars and the problem of escalation, the Premier stated:

> There have been local wars, and they may occur again in the future, but opportunities for imperialists to unleash these wars too are becoming fewer and fewer. A small imperialist war, regardless of which imperialist begins it, may grow into a world thermonuclear rocket war. We must therefore combat world wars and local wars.[2]

Having thus eliminated the probabilities but not the possibilities of general nuclear war and limited war, Khrushchev turned to the subject of "wars of national liberation" within the developing areas of Asia, Africa, and Latin America. He emphasized the importance to the Sino-Soviet bloc of the success of the "anti-imperialist" movements in these regions and he pledged aid to them as an "international duty" of all Communists. Referring to internal wars of national liberation, he said:

Can such wars flare up in the future? They can. Can there be such uprisings? There can. But these are wars which are national uprisings. In other words can conditions be created where a people will lose their patience and rise in arms? They can. What is the attitude of the Marxists toward such uprisings? A most positive one. These uprisings must not be identified with wars among states, with local wars, since in these uprisings the people are fighting for implementation of their right for self-determination, for independent social and national development. These are uprisings against rotten reactionary regimes, against the colonizers. The Communists fully support such just wars and march in the front rank with the peoples waging liberation struggles.[3]

After pointing out the existence of Communist parties in nearly fifty countries of Asia, Africa, and Latin America and stating that these parties alone could apply the theories of Marxism-Leninism best suited to their nations' needs, Khrushchev concluded by saying that the Soviets are "working for history." In other words, Communist doctrine prescribes active Soviet involvement in insurgency wars, "wars of national liberation," in the developing areas to insure success and expedite the inevitable flow of history.

The American View—President Kennedy's 1961 "State of the Union" address demonstrated American concern for, and the nature of the American response to, the special politico-military problems that have emerged from the nuclear stalemate situation:

. . . our strength may be tested at many levels. We intend to have at all times the capacity to resist non-nuclear or limited attacks—as a complement to our nuclear capacity, not as a substitute. We have rejected any all-or-nothing posture which would leave no choice but inglorious retreat or unlimited retaliation.[4]

In a later major policy speech in Chicago on February 17, 1962, Secretary of Defense Robert McNamara revealed an unusual interest in Premier Khrushchev's speech of January

6, 1961. The national liberation war theory advanced in that speech, he felt, "might well be one of the most important policy declarations in the '60s by any world leader."[5] Secretary McNamara elaborated on this theme in a prepared statement presented to the House Committee on Appropriations on the occasion of the hearings on the budget for the Department of Defense in early 1962:

So long as we maintain the kind of retaliatory forces possessed by SAC and Navy Polaris that tend to make global war, and even local wars, unprofitable for the USSR, we will continue to deter them from starting such wars. Indeed, to the extent we deter the Soviet Union from initiating these larger wars, we may anticipate even greater efforts on their part in the sublimited war area. Conflict, as Mr. Molotov so rightly pointed out, is a cardinal tenet of Communist doctrine.[6]

With a little more precision, Roger Hilsman (while serving as the State Department Director of Research and Intelligence) put it this way: ". . . the Communists have found what they regard as *a new chink in our armor*. The new tactic is internal war. . . ."[7] (Italics added.)

It is apparent that the United States fully appreciates the impact of the thermonuclear stalemate upon the Soviet Union's and, to a lesser degree, the Chinese Communists' offensive operations against elements of the Western Camp.

The Chinese Communist View—Official pronouncements from Peiping do not indicate that the Chinese Communist leadership fully appreciates the impact of thermonuclear weapons upon the East-West conflict, but it is significant to note that the Communist Party of China, in the lead article of the *People's Daily*, December 31, 1962, strongly endorses full support for national liberation wars.

The more the national liberation movements and the revolutionary struggles of the people develop, the better for the defence of world peace. The Socialist countries, the Communists of all countries, and all the peace-loving people of the world must resolutely support the national liberation movements and all the revolutionary struggles of the peoples and must resolutely support wars of national liberation and peoples' revolutionary wars.[8]

In assessing Communist China's commitment or non-commitment to the concept of insurgency warfare, it must be noted that Mao Tse-tung is the self-proclaimed father of modern guerrilla-insurgency warfare. Communist China gave substantial assistance to the Vietminh forces in their insurgency war against the French in contiguous Indochina; the Peiping regime also gave limited support to the Communist (HUK-HMB) insurgency forces and the Communist MRLA (Malayan Races Liberation Army) guerrillas in the non-contiguous Philippine Republic and Malayan Federation respectively. Finally, China's lack of substantial long-range airlift and sealift capabilities compels her to resort to the sponsorship of self-sustaining guerrilla-insurgency warfare in noncontiguous states if she is to remain on the offensive. The Chinese occupation of Tibet and the 1962 campaign against India, while overt military operations, were directed against contiguous and politically uncommitted developing states.

The ideological schism between China and the Soviet Union over the nature of total war and its inevitability seems to dictate that the former's explicit endorsement of insurgency warfare will be somewhat weaker and less encompassing than the latter's. As the analysis above suggests, however, there are many indicators which strongly suggest that Communist China in fact views sponsored insurgency warfare as an important means of pursuing foreign policy goals that involve noncontiguous developing states and are directly related to the West-Communist East conflict.

Internal Instability

The last general factor to be considered, internal instability, is a compound of conditional subfactors. Before discussing the more important of these subfactors, we must appreciate the two-phased nature of instability in the developing nations. The first phase is a direct consequence of the exposure of

primitive or technologically less advanced cultures to the conditions and values of the economically and technically more
advanced countries. Western colonization and World War II
served as the great vehicles of this exposure. From this meeting comes the "revolution of rising expectations" and the avid
desire for rapid and dramatic change, at least among the educated minority. The second phase begins when a particular
society moves from merely desiring change to experiencing it
with shattering impact upon its sociocultural fabric.

The Problem of Cultural Adjustment—This factor is most
pronounced during Phase Two instability. Then the élite
groups of a new state attempt a mutation of indigenous culture and instead actually start a metamorphosis. Because of
the interlocking nature of a culture, a change in one aspect
will inevitably and quite rapidly affect the total culture.[9] Once
technological innovations are made in a preindustrial society,
a chain reaction of expanded and largely *unexpected* change
occurs. The additional tension thus created dislocates the entire system.

Poverty—Most underdeveloped countries are plagued by
agrarian subsistence economies. The nations that produce for
export, either through agriculture or extractive industries,
usually have only one or two marketable commodities. As
world prices for their commodities fluctuate, the majority of
the population moves from starvation to subsistence and back
again.

These factors are aggravated by, if not directly caused by,
absentee land ownership. In some states the great bulk of the
population is deprived of the dignity of owning the land it
works. They are thus deprived of the hope for a better life for
their children. Poverty is all-pervasive so that, exposed to
revolutionary ideologies, such societies become highly unstable.

Still another economic problem is born as Westernization
takes hold. The gap increases in the living standards between
the urban indigenous élite and the majority of the rural popu-

lation. As this becomes more apparent to rural sectors, the poorer farmers start drifting into the city to better their lives. The limited capacity of the developing industrial sector for absorbing additional labor often forces these farmers to become the disenchanted, unemployed slum dwellers. The cause of instability then becomes a problem of the distribution of the new resources and benefits derived from modernization. The formerly external versus internal conflict between wealth and poverty now becomes essentially internal.

The population explosion also complicates the economic outlook. A rapidly increasing population combined with declining standards of living in nations already beset by poverty makes an already dangerous situation worse.

Nationalism—This promises to be the panacea to the oppression of the masses in the underdeveloped areas that are or have been exploited by Western nations. Unlike traditional nationalism of the West, this ideology of the developing states is exceedingly socially conscious. Independence and the creation of a strong nation-state have become the *sine qua non* for socioeconomic development.

Nationalism at first does serve some constructive purposes. It furnishes a people with a sense of independent worth and self-respect and provides a cohesive force during the replacement of traditional tribal or communal bonds shattered by the impact with Western states. After independence has been gained, nationalism causes a great potential widening of the social and political horizons of the people.

This non-Western nationalism also has several failings. First, it is essentially an "anti" ideology, and all that is bad is unrealistically attributed to the central object of this "anti" feeling. Second, this ideology fails to determine the political and economic institutions the people need after they have organized themselves into a nation-state. Also, as with economic modernization, the urban élite of the developing countries tend to be the principal if not the exclusive beneficiaries of early nationalism. These benefits come in forms of political power, social prestige, and material betterment. Hence the urban-rural conflict extends into the sociopolitical as well as the economic realm and promotes further instability.

Dissident Groups (non-Communist)—One group of natural dissidents in any state undergoing the modernization process is quite obviously the beneficiaries of the old order. Most developing states also appear to be plagued by extremely active dissidences based on racial division, religious divisions, social class antagonisms, and politico-military rivalries. For example, the small and troubled state of Laos is a complex ethnic mosaic of the valley-dwelling Buddhist Lao: their linguistic cousins, the tribal Tai; the aboriginal Kha; upland tribes such as the Meo and Yao (originating in China); and smaller urban minority groups of Chinese, Vietnamese, Indians, Pakistanis, and Europeans. Malaya, Indonesia, and the Philippines (to a much lesser extent) have been troubled by their "Chinese problems." Burma is still plagued by the Karen problem, and the Central Congolese government is troubled by dissident tribal groups and the political mutiny of Katanga. Pagans in the newly emergent states of central and east Africa have strained relations with their northern Moslem fellow countrymen. The pathetic forgotten Indians of the South American states are becoming restive and desirous of the ways of life followed by their mestizo and European countrymen.

Until these centrifugal forces can be eliminated and most hopefully transformed into centripetal forces, neither economic development nor political stability can be meaningfully postulated as an attainable objective for a developing state.

The Élites—This element creates instability in two ways. As already mentioned, the traditional élite can form a "dissident" group trying to hold back any march toward modernity. Or else the modern élite can so control the developmental process that only they receive its immediate benefits. Such restrictions—if the populace has already been exposed to the fruits of modernity—can cause frustrations strong enough to create forces designed to remove power from the incumbent élite. In many of the old as well as the new nation-states the institutions for an orderly transfer of political power do not exist or have not solidified. Competition for high political office among factions of the élite often leads to *coups d'état.* Even though these *coups* result only in transitory instability, a succession of them can have an unnerving effect upon the national political process.

Deficient Civil Administration—The rather sudden departure of the colonial administrators and professionals from Africa and Asia in the decade and a half since World War II has created a civil-administrative vacuum in most of the newly formed states. This abrupt removal of the old control mechanisms (with the possible exception of a few British and French colonies), which once brought stability and orderly processes to these areas, has resulted in long-term problems. Into the vacuum have rushed native administrators who had been trained, for the most part, only as literate clerks and accountants and minor government functionaries.

A parallel problem can be found in some Latin American states which cast off their colonial ties in the early nineteenth century. In some of these states, selfish, tyrannical élites control the government, and corruption and police brutality are normal modes of operation.

Whether such civil-administrative deficiencies are the products of the "accidents" of history or the "design" of corrupt tyrannies, they induce a significant degree of actual and potential instability into the governance of the developing states.

The Disenchanted Intellectuals—Despite the shortage of administrators and professionals in most developing states, groups of unemployed intellectuals exist in a few underdeveloped nations—for example, Pakistan, India, Egypt, Korea, and Burma.[10] Many Latin American states—specializing in the so-called political universities rather than the North American type of professional universities—experience this problem among their recent college graduates. There are also the disenchanted and disillusioned intellectuals who may hold important positions in government or in the nonpublic sectors of national life. They may be disenchanted with the apparent inefficiency of a mixed economy or impatient with the democratic process.

The presence of unemployed, disenchanted intellectuals presents a potentially dangerous problem to a new state attempting to establish the best government for its national society. These intellectuals form the possible leadership elements of insurgent as well as legal opposition.

Indigenous Communist Movements—Communists in the underdeveloped nations hold two aces in psychological warfare. Inherent in the mental attitude in the politically conscious peoples of these areas has been, and continues to be, a resentment both of the West's "exploitation" (real or imagined) of their indigenous resources and of their technological inferiority. Native Communists have capitalized on this by readily portraying the USSR both as a symbol of resistance to imperialism and as a model of self-directed and rapid industrialization. With the Chinese Communist victory, another model of resistance and internal reconstruction via the "Communist way" is being offered for emulation.

It is obvious that, because of this initial empathy gained by small Communist cadres with the politically conscious indigenous peoples, it is not too difficult to establish a Communist party in most underdeveloped states. However, because of religious considerations, sociocultural conditions, or a repressive anti-Communist government, the size of these parties may remain small and their overt activities may be restricted if not completely curtailed.

The indigenous Communist party will follow either a hard or a soft strategy, depending upon internal and international conditions. Pursuit of a soft strategy may include possibilities ranging from attempts to influence a neutralist government to become more anti-Western to legal efforts to gain power in the actual government of a developing state. The hard strategic alternatives may range from subversion and infiltration through *coup d'état* to expansive overt insurgency warfare. It can reasonably be assumed that the native Communist parties organize themselves (and equip themselves as far as is possible) in these developing states so that they can pursue simultaneously either one of the general strategic alternatives and in some cases both strategies.

This review of the general problem of instability, although brief, nevertheless points out its very complex nature. This problem is dominated neither by economic nor by Communist elements *per se*. Instead, as American policy-makers increasingly recognize, it is a complex social, political, psychological, economic, and ideological phenomenon of the developing areas. Obviously any counterinsurgency plan will also have to be an equally complex mixture.

Communist insurgency warfare during the 1965–1975 period will continue to be a complex function of three general variables: conflicting ideology, which has both worldwide and local dimensions; strategic nuclear stalemate, which has a world dimension only; and internal instability. The last, while primarily a local dimension, is in itself a complex multifaceted phenomenon. Because of this, a strategic planner of Western counterinsurgency operations is forced to throw out any notions of "quick-fix" plans and unidimensional (for example, economics or military dominated) solutions. He is compelled to scrutinize each insurgency by calling upon virtually all the disciplines of the social sciences. Once a Communist-sponsored insurgency has been identified, the planner is compelled to view this conflict within the microcosm of the specifically affected area and the macrocosm of the international political arena.[11]

3

The Evolution of Communist
Theory on Insurgency Warfare:
An Historical Perspective

Antecedents to Communist insurgency warfare can be found throughout the pages of ancient and modern history. Infiltration and subversion are described in the Bible and in ancient Greek histories. Two classic examples before the birth of Christ can be found in the "Trojan Horse" (1000 B.C.) and "Seven Against Thebes" (Peloponnesian Wars, 431–404 B.C.) episodes. More recent and pertinent examples are the activities of the OSS and British SOE in occupied Europe of 1942–1945, the exploits of the German forces under the command of Colonel Skorzeny during World War II, and the operations of the Tudeh party in post-World War II Iran.

Infiltration and subversion tactics throughout the ages have been refined to meet the changing environment. Today they constitute the introductory stage of Communist insurgency warfare in the underdeveloped areas.

Antecedents of guerrilla warfare—the principal mode of conflict in two of the four stages of Communist insurgency—can be found in ancient as well as in modern history. The Old Testament describes the guerrilla campaign of the Maccabees against the Syrian armies. Both irregulars and regulars took part in these military operations. The employment of small bands of regulars for delaying and harassing actions has long been termed the Fabian theory or tactic of warfare in tribute to Fabius Maximus's unorthodox but successful campaign to divert Hannibal's superior force from Rome.[1]

The term *guerrilla warfare* did not become a part of the military vocabulary until after Napoleon's victorious sweep through Spain in 1807–1808. The Spanish army was dissolved in defeat and then reorganized into small independent units capable of fighting only limited actions. Hence the Spanish diminutive suffix was added to the vernacular term for war, *guerra,* and thus the term *guerrilla* was coined to describe the continuing war against France.

Guerrilla units, essentially irregular forces, sometimes grouped around small core cadres of regulars, and became prominent, though not dominant, elements in many European and American wars during the nineteenth century. To cite but a few examples: the Cossack and partisan operations against the French columns retreating from Moscow, 1812; Greek partisan revolutionary operations against the Ottoman Empire, 1821–1827; Mexican guerrilla operations against Scott's movements in the Mexico City Campaign, 1847; General Mosby's partisan operations in the Shenandoah Valley, 1862–1863; Bosnian-Herzegovinian guerrilla operations against the Austro-Hungarian army, 1878–1882; and Boer operations against the British in South Africa, 1898. In the twentieth century, before the end of World War II, guerrilla warfare again played a prominent role in military operations. Arabian irregular warfare (led by the Englishman T. E. Lawrence) against the Turks in the Near East during World War I is the most notable example. The guerrilla-terrorist activities of the Zionists in Palestine, 1917–1945, and the numerous anti-German partisan campaigns in occupied Europe, 1940–1945, are additional examples.

The heart of guerrilla warfare as it has evolved during the

modern period is the complete "politicization" of military combat; therefore, it is not surprising to find that its first significant appearance in military-theoretical literature is in Book VI of Clausewitz's *On War*. In Chapter 26, "Volksbewaffnung," the author enumerates five general conditions for the successful pursuit of guerrilla warfare: (1) operations must be conducted in the interior of a country, (2) war cannot hinge on a single battle, (3) the theater of war must be extensive, (4) the national character must support the war, and (5) the country must have irregular, difficult, and inaccessible terrain features.[2] Clausewitz, however, appears to view guerrilla warfare as an ancillary military methodology. He does not consider it the proper option if the alternative establishment of a viable regular force is realistically achievable. Although he indicates that guerrilla warfare must always be tactically offensive, he also states that it will naturally be strategically defensive.

T. E. Lawrence, on the contrary, contributes the additional dimension of strategic offense. And contrary to the Clausewitzian view, Lawrence asserts that the selection of guerrilla warfare to achieve a certain general objective may be, under certain circumstances, the proper alternative even if regular forces can be created.

Lawrence's proposition that the true objective of guerrilla warfare is not necessarily fighting contradicts the then (1916–1918) universally accepted dictum that the ethic of modern war is to seek the enemy's army, his center of power, and to destroy it in battle. For Lawrence, the first principle of guerrilla warfare is one of detachment from the enemy. He will contain the enemy by posing the silent threat of selective tactical strikes from every point on the compass. A corollary of this principle is perfect intelligence of the enemy's movements and strength. This intelligence has to come from a friendly, or at least apathetic, populace. His second principle is to destroy the enemy's most vulnerable source of strength.

As it pertained to the Turkish Army, this was war matériel and not troops, because equipment was less plentiful than were men.

The work of Lawrence, despite his successes, has been appreciated more in Russia and China than among his own people. Accepting Clausewitz's dictum that "war is a continuation of politics by other means," the Communists emphasize the political facet of guerrilla war and then graft socioeconomic and ideological concepts to Lawrence's military tactics. Thus over the years they have formulated a theory of Communist insurgency warfare.

The Soviet Contribution

Before we discuss the contributions of Russian Communist leaders to the current theory of Communist insurgency warfare, we must note that the actual roots of this theory can quite logically be traced to Marx and Engels. These founding fathers of Communism, in considering the manner in which their revolution would unfold, looked to insurgency warfare of a conspiratorial, sociopolitical, and unorthodox nature as the logical solution. Marx went so far as to claim that only by unorthodox methods of warfare can a weaker force actually defeat a stronger one.[3] One can easily see here the germination of the theory that we shall now discuss.

The most important Russian contributor to this theory is Lenin. His endorsement of the tactic of infiltration-subversion is found in most of his major writings. Not so well known, however, are his endorsements of principles of operations that are fundamental to the conduct of guerrilla war. For example:

. . . to accept battle at a time when it is obviously advantageous to the enemy and not to us is a crime: and those political leaders of the revolutionary class who are unable to "tack, to manoeuvre, to compromise" in order to avoid an obviously disadvantageous battle, are good for nothing.

We have never rejected terror on principle, nor can we do so. Terror is a form of military operation that may be usefully applied, or may even be essential in certain moments.[4]

Lenin's definitive work dealing specifically with "partisan" (guerrilla) warfare is *Partisanskaya Voina*. This essay, which originally appeared on October 13, 1906, in the newspaper *Proletari,* describes partisan warfare as a combination of terrorism, robbery, and ambush to support the revolutionary struggle.[5] In defending the adoption of partisan warfare by the Bolshevik wing of the Social Democratic Party, Lenin states:

. . . Marxism does not tie the movement to any particular combat method. It recognizes the possibility that struggle may assume the most variegated forms. For that matter, Marxism does not "invent" those forms of struggle. It merely organizes the tactics of strife and renders them suitable for general use.[6]

Lenin sees a somewhat limited set of objectives for the pursuit of this type of warfare. His first stated objective is the assassination of officials; the second is the confiscation of money from the government and well-endowed private persons. The assassinations are to spread terror into the ranks of the government. The money is to be the principal source of funds for the purchase of arms and for other expenditures related to the preparation for the eventual uprising.

The founder of Bolshevism, in describing the changing nature of the Russian Communist revolution, introduces the concept of protracted revolutionary conflict and urges the party to create suitable organizations to lead the masses during such a difficult period of extended combat:

The enemies of our revolution have but few followers among the people, but as the fight develops, the opponents are getting better and better organized and are gaining support from reactionary groups of the bourgeoisie. Thus, it is natural and unavoidable that in such periods . . . the uprising cannot assume the traditional form of a single blow limited to a very short time and a very small area (*i.e.,* not a single one thrust insurrection in the capital against the seat of government). [Under such circumstances] it is natural and unavoidable that the uprising assume the *higher and more complicated form of a protracted civil war enmeshing the entire country*. Such a war must be conceived as a series of a few big battles, separated by comparatively long intervals, and a large number of small engagements, which take place during these interim periods . . . then the task of social democracy is to create organizations most suitable to leading masses both in the big battles and, so far as practical, in smaller actions. . . . The SDP must educate and prepare its organizations in such a way that *they will not fail to exploit opportunities through which the strengths of the opponent can be sapped*.[7] (Italics added.)

In this protracted conflict Lenin sees the role of partisan warfare as solely a secondary and incidental part of the entire revolutionary process. This operational restriction and the somewhat modest objectives Lenin prescribed for partisan operations have been considerably modified by current Communist theorists on insurgency warfare. The necessity for such modifications, however, appears to have been foreseen by Lenin:

Marxism asks that the various types of struggle be analyzed within their historical framework. To discuss conflict outside of its historical and concrete setting is to misunderstand elementary dialectic materialism. At various junctures of economic evolution, and depending on changing political, national, cultural, social and other conditions, differing types of struggle may become important and even predominant.[8]

Lenin's successor, Stalin, was a professional insurgent of the highest (or, more appropriately, *lowest*) caliber. During his early life, he led an exciting career as a guerrilla-revolutionist in the Caucasus Mountains. In referring to Stalin, Trotsky writes, "Well organized violence seems to him the shortest distance between two points . . . he is a kind of opportunist with a bomb. . . ."[9] Stalin's major contribution to modern Communist insurgency warfare theory can be found in his "Marxism and the National Question." This essay contains the germ for later Communist ideas about mobilizing colonial peoples against capitalist powers.

During Stalin's regime, a doctrine for guerrilla warfare was published, entitled simply *The Russian Partisan Directive of*

1933. A special theory of guerrilla warfare emerges from Soviet endeavors to implement this doctrine after the German occupation of the western USSR. This theory states that, to be effective, Soviet guerrillas operating behind enemy lines will have to complete two separate but compatible missions. They will have to harass the occupation forces and inflict maximum damage on communications and logistics installations. *This is a military and economic mission.* Then, in occupied areas, they will have to maintain the allegiance of the Russian population to the USSR and to its Communist system. *This is clearly a political and psychological mission.* Hence the idea of a guerrilla being more than a military instrument is registered in Soviet Communist theory on warfare.

The Contributions of Mao Tse-tung

Undoubtedly the one individual who has contributed most to the development of the theory of modern Communist insurgency warfare is the Chinese patriarch, Mao Tse-tung. He has been a perfector of the traditional dimensions of this composite theory, a prolific originator of its new dimensions, and a masterful organizer of both.

Mao's major writings, which contain the crux of this theory, *On the Rectification of Incorrect Ideas in the Party* (1929), *Strategic Problems of China's Revolutionary War* (1936), *Yu Chi Chan* (loosely translated as *Guerrilla War,* 1937), and *On the Protracted Conflict* (1938), reflect the contributions made by fellow Communists—Marx, Engels, Lenin, and Stalin—and by such non-Communists as the ancient military theorist Sun Tzu and the modern theorists Clausewitz and Lawrence. His writings also reflect the results of practical experimentation in the problems of resistance and insurgency operations initiated by an "inferior" force in a vast underdeveloped area against modern-equipped but "reactionary" foreign and indigenous armies. These experiments began in the disastrous 1926 "Autumn Harvest" uprisings in south China (Hunan and Kiangsi regions) and continued through the "Long March" and the "Isolation Period" in Shensi Province during the years 1934–1936. They were continued against the Japanese occupiers from 1937 to 1945, and the "scientific" fruits of these experiments were then directed against the Kuomintang, which collapsed in 1949 and thus ushered in the birth of the People's Republic of China.

The most theoretical element that Mao accepts from the Communist cultural heritage is the historical necessity of war as the proper vehicle for "the Revolution."[10] The significant corollary—the importance of the people in such an enterprise—comes quite naturally to him as it had to his predecessors who expressed some interest in studying the problems of people's war. Mao, however, systematizes these studies, introduces indigenous ingredients, and adds a heavy tactical operational doctrine to their more esoteric findings. He does not feel particularly constrained to follow exactly the prescriptions of the Russians, Lenin and Stalin, despite the fact that he pays courteous tribute to them in his writings. He declares quite bluntly on numerous occasions during the 1930's that Russian theoretical contributions and experiences cannot simply be transferred to the Chinese scene because, as he states:

> There are a great number of conditions special to the Chinese revolution and the Chinese Red Army . . . laws of war and military directives in the Soviet Union embody the special characteristics of the civil war and the Red Army of the Soviet Union; if we copy them and apply them mechanically and allow no change whatsoever, it will also be like whittling down our feet to fit the shoes, and we shall be defeated.[11]

Mao's contributions to Communist insurgency warfare theory can be most fruitfully analyzed if three foci are established. The first focus, and the one easiest to isolate, is the philosophical genesis of his contributions. The second and third foci are the strategic and tactical prescriptions of these contributions.

The philosophical core of Mao's theoretical postulations is his principle of the "unity of opposites." This is probably a political-military adaptation of the ancient Chinese philosophical concept of *Yin-Yang* which is concerned with the reciprocal and endless interaction of direct opposites. An important and pertinent postulate of this theory is that there is concealed weakness in strength.[12] There are several examples of the application of this principle to warfare. It is a weakness of guerrillas that they operate in small bands which can be completely destroyed in minor skirmishes. Because they do operate as small units, they are capable of rapid and secret movement behind enemy lines. In conventional operations, dispersion invites destruction. In guerrilla war, however, dispersion is necessary in order both to confuse the enemy and to project the image of large guerrilla forces. Finally, the guerrillas' "front line" of operation is the enemy's rear.[13]

Mao applies a slight modification of this principle in his redevelopment of the strength ratios factor between opposing military forces. Although his redevelopment process does not exactly call for the computation of opposites, it does call for the placement of near opposites into the same category for purposes of calculating relative strength differentials. The enemy's military and economic strength is placed in the same category as the insurgents' manpower and mental attitudes. "Weapons are an important factor in war, but not the decisive one; it is man and not material that counts."[14] Continuing this type of near-opposite substitution process within specific categories of military strength, he opposes airpower with excellent intelligence, tanks with propaganda, mechanized forces with intelligence, and space (area) and industrial mobilization with political mobilization.

A key oppositional postulation is space against time.[15] The theoretical concepts of protracted warfare and the cellular evolution of the stages of insurgency warfare both stem from this postulation. Mao is quite willing to exchange space for time; the more difficult the terrain, the longer will this exchange process take. Time—time above all—is what the insurgency feeds upon. It is through time that a technologically inferior force can so organize and indoctrinate the populace that it will become in essence the collective base of this insurgency. It is from this base that the insurgent forces will derive a growing strength that will ultimately permit them to destroy the incumbent government's modern army.

Mao describes the three stages of such growth and prescribes that an insurgency movement, to insure victory, will have to pass through all three stages. The first stage, the *strategic defensive,* is characterized by the initiation of insurgency by small armed forces who then make a *gradual* but heroic retreat before the massive retaliation of the incumbent's modern army. This retreat results in a loss of space but a gaining of time. During this stage the insurgents should never permit or submit to positional warfare. Their primary objective is survival over time. Thus the enemy's frustrations will multiply because they have been denied significant victories.

The first stage then slips into the second stage, *stalemate.* Survival is still the primary objective, and the guerrilla tactic of quick strike and quick retreat is the principal mode of military operations for the insurgents. The sense of futility among the incumbent's troops and on his home front continues to grow, and the casualties and expense of the military effort have a generally debilitating effect upon the morale of the entire incumbent camp. The war actually reaches a state of equilibrium with the insurgents controlling little land but still maintaining a position of tactical initiative. As the incumbents' morale declines, that of the insurgents rises, and a program of expansion of forces and an increase in operations begins.

With this increase in the frequency and spacial scope of insurgent-guerrilla warfare comes the initiation of large-scale mobile warfare and the creation of regular army units. Stage three, *the strategic offensive,* begins as these regular army units grow in size and positional warfare begins to dominate the mode of conflict. Guerrilla warfare becomes supplementary. The regular insurgent army, assisted by the guerrillas, then pursues the war to a successful termination.

Because guerrilla warfare dominates the first two stages of Maoist insurgency and remains an important supplement to regular army operations in stage three, Mao devotes much of his writing to this type of military action. Most important is his exposition of the six strategic principles "which are essential for the conservation and development of our strength and the destruction of the enemy" during the three-stage development of the insurgency.[16]

1. On our own initiative, with flexibility and according to our own plan, carry out offensives in a defensive war, battles of quick decision in a protracted war, and exterior line operations within interior line operation.
2. Coordination with regular warfare.
3. The establishment of base areas.
4. Strategic defensive and strategic offensive in guerrilla warfare.
5. Development into mobile warfare.
6. Relationship of commands.[17]

In elaborating on the first principle, Mao's discussions of its strategic value rapidly spill into the area of tactics. (This is also the case with his subsequent expansions of the remaining five points.) Mao emphasizes over and over again the importance of speed, of surprise, and of maintaining the offensive:

In every war the opponents strive with each other for the initiative, since it means freedom of action for an army. The initiative results from correct estimations of the situation (of both the enemy and ourselves) as well as correct military and political dispositions.[18]

When discussing the problems of dispersion and concentration and of the capabilities of guerrilla leaders, Mao uses an analogy of the good fisherman who is able to place his nets for the greatest possible catch but also can pull them out if adverse situations develop. The fisherman, he continues, must have in advance a full awareness of the depth of the water, the strength of the current, and the presence of any obstructions. Just as the fisherman controls his nets through his lead ropes, so the guerrilla leader maintains contact with and control over his dispersed units. "As the fisherman must change his position, so must the guerrilla commander. Dispersion, concentration, constant change of position—it is in these ways that guerrillas employ their strength."[19]

Mao's concluding comments in his discussion of the first principle emphasize the importance of careful and detailed planning for all guerrilla operations. He makes the strong point that each battle planned must be viewed as a part of the entire campaign, a part of the organic whole. In addition, "if a battle prejudices the entire campaign rather than benefits it, then victory in such a battle can only be considered a defeat."[20] In this last statement, Mao is obviously elevating the political dimension of a battle over its purely military and tactical aspects. In other words, a tactical military victory that prejudices the cause of the insurgents, as viewed by the general populace, is for all practical purposes a strategic defeat.

Mao's elaboration of the second strategic principle is quite brief. He notes that there are three types of cooperation or coordination of guerrillas with regular forces: "strategic," "tactical," and "battle." Guerrilla operations that range the enemy's rear, harass him, and encourage popular resistance are cooperative in a strategic manner. Guerrilla actions that support a regional commander and his operations are tactical. Mao emphasizes the importance of close cooperation in this joint activity lest both forces be maneuvered by the enemy into untenable positions from which neither force can move to aid the other. As it relates to guerrilla cooperation and coordination at the "battle level," the Chinese leader prescribes that guerrillas disrupt enemy transport and serve as intelligence collectors. They should automatically assume these duties even if they have not received precise instructions from the commander of the regular force.[21]

The third principle, the establishment of base areas, is considered especially important by Mao. "A guerrilla base may

be defined as an area strategically located, in which the guerrillas can carry out their duties of training, self-preservation,
and development."[22] He then states that fundamental to any
guerrilla movements is the ability of such forces to fight without a rear area. Being a realist as well as an optimist, however, he concludes that this fundamental characteristic does
not imply that guerrillas could or should exist and function
over a long period of time without the development of base
areas.

Mao categorizes base areas according to their terrain features: first, mountain bases; second, plains bases; last, river,
lake, and bay bases. After pointing out the advantages of
mountain bases, he notes that even though plains bases are
generally unfavorable, small temporary bases can be formed
if the populace is friendly. In further developing his third
principle, Mao distinguishes between "guerrilla base areas" and
"guerrilla areas." It is important to appreciate this distinction
because it illuminates the basic strategic concept of offense in
his prescriptions:

> In a guerrilla war conducted in the enemy's rear, guerrilla areas
> must be distinguished from guerrilla base areas. Areas which are
> surrounded by the enemy but whose central parts are not occupied
> by him are ready-made base areas where the guerrilla units can
> conveniently develop guerrilla warfare. Areas which guerrillas
> could not completely occupy but could only constantly harass and
> attack are not yet guerrilla base areas but only guerrilla areas.
> Such guerrilla areas will be transformed into base areas when they
> have gone through the necessary processes in a guerrilla war,
> that is, when a large number of enemy troops have been annihi-
> lated or defeated, the puppet regime destroyed, the activity of the
> people called forth, popular organizations formed, the people's
> armed forces developed, and political power established. . . . [There
> are] three categories: first, guerrilla base areas controlled by our
> guerrilla units and our organs of political power; secondly, areas
> in the grip of imperialism and the puppet regime; and thirdly,
> intermediate zones contested by both sides, i.e., guerrilla areas.[23]

The remainder of Mao's elaborations of the third principle
deals with the establishment and development of base areas.
The achievement of a feeling of brotherhood between the guer-

rillas and the populace is considered of primary importance. Once this support is acquired, then the creation of mass organizations of workers, peasants, youth, women, and others begins, and local militias are formed and trained. Government is established, and taxation is initiated to support the Communist-guerrilla administration. Confiscation for purposes of acquiring funds is explicitly forbidden except in the case of businesses run by traitors. Mao closes this particular discussion by prescribing a rhythmic evolutionary process for base areas. "At times, we must emphasize the development and extension of base areas; at other times, the organization, training, or equipment of the people."[24]

The fourth principle, strategic defensive and strategic offensive, has already been discussed in the context of the stages of the development of a Maoist insurgency war. The fifth principle, development into mobile warfare, has also been discussed briefly in this same context. Elaboration, however, is desirable.

Mao considers the development of mobile warfare absolutely essential. Nevertheless, he points out that guerrilla units should not be disbanded as the regular armed forces grow in size:

The fourth strategic problem in the guerrilla war is its development into mobile war. For the transformation of the guerrilla units now engaged in a guerrilla war into a Regular army which can wage a mobile war, two conditions are required: increase in their numbers and improvement in their quality.

The development of guerrilla warfare into mobile warfare does not mean the abandonment of guerrilla warfare but the gradual formation in the midst of an extensively developed guerrilla warfare of a main force capable of conducting a mobile war, round which there should still be numerous guerrilla forces carrying on extensive guerrilla operations.[25]

The strategy prescribed once this regular force has been created and trained is that of employing the main forces in mobile warfare over an extended, shifting, and indefinite front. This strategy depends for success on a high degree of

mobility and flexibility and features swift attack and withdrawal, swift concentration and dispersal. The advocated concentration of force is based on the principle of guaranteeing
an absolute or relative superiority on the battlefield. Mao essentially prescribes the regularization and expansion of guerrilla units and the continued maintenance of the tactical
principles of guerrilla warfare. This condition is to persist until
the regular forces are strong enough to wage positional war
on local fronts where the tactical situation favors such dispo-
sition and action.

The sixth and final principle, relationship of commands,
is only briefly treated in Mao's elaborations on these six cardinal strategic elements. He re-emphasizes the requirements
for coordination of "independent" guerrilla unit operations at
a zonal level in order to insure the effectiveness of these
operations as they pertain to the activities of other guerrilla
units and also to regular troop units operating within a particular zone.

As it pertains to guerrilla base areas, the command is to be
centralized for strategic purposes and decentralized for tactical purposes. Each area is to be divided into districts and these
in turn into subdistricts. Each subdivision will have a commander appointed from above. General plans will be made at
higher levels of command, but the nature of the implementing
actions will be determined by inferior commanders. In sum-
ming up proper command relationship, Mao concludes, "In a
word, proper guerrilla policy will provide for unified strategy
and independent activity."[26]

These six principles, even in their elaborated form, do not
explicitly or implicitly provide the full core content of Mao's
writings on Communist insurgency warfare. To complete the
picture, some other key principles, strategic and tactical, will
be outlined.

1. *Relationships between guerrillas and the people.* In
prescribing the nature of this relationship, Mao codifies for

guerrilla operations the "Three Rules and Eight Remarks of the Eighth Route Army":

Rules—All actions are subject to command; do not steal from the people; be neither selfish nor unjust.
Remarks—Replace the door when you leave the house; roll up the bedding in which you have slept; be courteous; be honest in your transactions; return what you borrow; replace what you break; do not bathe in the presence of women; do not without authority search the pocketbooks of those you arrest.[27]

Mao sees in the people not only the capability for survival of his weak guerrilla forces but also the potential hope of ultimate victory. Pursuing his now somewhat trite analogy of the people as water and the guerrillas as fish, he states in the *Protracted Conflict*, "With the common people of the whole country mobilized, we shall create a vast sea of humanity and drown the enemy in it. . . ."[28] It is obvious that Mao holds military salvation, ideologically speaking, as a direct concomitant of the political conversion of the masses.[29]

2. *The "politicization" of the military forces.* This principle applies to all troops, guerrillas, and members of the regular army once it has been established. Mao stated this principle, one of his earliest postulations on insurgency war, in 1929. His declaration is:

When the Red Army fights, it fights not merely for the sake of fighting, but to agitate the masses, to organize them, to arm them, and to help them establish revolutionary political power; apart from such objectives, fighting loses its meaning and the Red Army the reason for its existence.[30]

Unlike the traditions within the Western military services—especially the Anglo-Saxon military establishments, which call for the "de-politicization" of the military—Mao prescribes the permeation of politics into the whole of military organization, training, and operations. In turning on these military figures in his ranks who subscribe to the traditional Western view, he states:

There are often military elements who "care for only military affairs but not politics." Such one-track minded military officers, ignoring the interconnection between politics and military affairs, must be made to understand the correct relationship between the two. All military actions are means to achieve certain political objectives while military action itself is a manifested form of politics. There are of course differences between political and military affairs, each with its special characteristics, but the one should not be disconnected and isolated from the other.[31]

Mao stipulates that political officers be assigned to all significant command levels. He also calls for an extensive political indoctrination program to be conducted at the base areas and on the march during rest breaks.

3. *"There are no decisive battles in guerrilla warfare."* This tactical principle not only permits retreat under unfavorable combat situations but actually prescribes retreat in all situations in which the guerrillas do not have local superiority. Mao stresses continually the importance of maintaining the aura of success for the guerrilla movement. Losses must be kept at a minimum. After a skirmish guerrillas carry off their wounded, and dead if possible, to preserve this aura in the eyes of the populace. Attacks must be made only when the insurgents have a local superiority of at least five to one. The very price of survival is caution, and the principle of caution is to be extolled and not deprecated during the guerrilla phase of Maoist insurgency warfare.

4. *Discipline in the guerrilla forces must be internally imposed.* While Mao notes the importance of discipline as the basis for effective military operations, he contends that the peculiarities of guerrilla warfare dictate that discipline have a democratic basis and that it be imposed from within, not a product of external compulsion. He states that a by-product of externally imposed discipline is the creation of a relationship of indifference to one another between the officers and the men. This situation is intolerable in guerrilla units. Mao thus prescribes that the officers be *of* the men and not *above* them. They must live under the same conditions as their

troops. Their true badge of distinction, and the element that instills a sense of self-imposed discipline in the men, is their intellectual superiority, demonstrated in their knowledge of Communist ideology and the tactical principles of guerrilla warfare. He concedes, however, that the nature of discipline within his regular armed forces will approach the conventional concepts of this unifying factor of military units.

5. *The value of propaganda.* The principal tactical objectives of guerrilla warfare are to harass the enemy and undermine his will to resist and, concurrently, to achieve an aura of military success for the guerrilla forces and so hearten the populace in its resistance to the incumbents. Obviously, propaganda activities can assist in achieving these objectives. Propaganda, as a consequence, is to be directed against the enemy in order to induce him to surrender or even to join the ranks of the insurgents. In this regard, Mao prescribes that captured prisoners be treated with consideration and their wounded be cared for. He states, "If we fail in these respects, we strengthen the solidarity of our enemy."[32]

Propaganda is to be directed at the people to portray the insurgents as the brave and self-sacrificing representatives of the oppressed masses. These masses are to be presented with a description of the Communist alternative way of life. They are to be told that this mode of living will occur only if the insurgents can defeat the incumbent "reactionary" government forces. Thus the aid of the masses is to be solicited through the promise of the fruits of victory. However, as victory is ultimately and inevitably assured because of the "ideological correctness" of the movement, the masses are led to believe that only a fool would stand in the way or refuse to support the insurgency movement.

It is of interest that Mao even goes so far as to prescribe the type of propaganda materials that guerrillas acquire:

Propaganda materials are very important. Every large guerrilla unit should have a printing press and a mimeograph stone. They must also have paper on which to print propaganda leaflets and notices. They must be supplied with chalk and large brushes. In guerrilla areas, there should be a printing press or a lead-type press.[33]

6. *Recruitment and local area operations.*   Mao indicates that the supply of weapons constitutes a most difficult logistics problem. Even though he advocates that "people's armories" be constructed in each guerrilla area, he makes it quite clear that captured enemy supplies will be a principal source of the guerrilla's war matériel.

When filling out the ranks of guerrilla units, Mao insists that these units operate on the principle that only volunteers are acceptable for service. As long as a person is willing to fight, his social position or condition should not preclude his enlistment.[34]

Somewhat related to filling the ranks of guerrilla units is Mao's prescription that these units operate only in their home area. This restriction of the geographic areas of operation of each unit insures the guerrillas of two principal advantages over the enemy—superior knowledge of terrain and superior claim to intelligence from the populace.

In summary, the fundamental thread that runs through Mao Tse-tung's writings on insurgency is the dual concept of adaptation to the realities of a given situation and transformation of conventional weaknesses into unconventional strengths. Because he accepts the ideological thesis of Marx, the inevitability of victory for socialism, he premises all designs for strategic and tactical actions on the assumption that time is on his side. He is willing to accept defeats; he is willing to see a developing insurgency slip back from an advanced stage to a preceding stage. This is explained away as "revolutionary flow."[35] As he sees it, it is obviously only a temporary setback because fundamental to all else is ultimate, inevitable victory. Therefore, his prescriptions, as read and analyzed by leaders of insurgent movements in other underdeveloped states, take on the aspect of scientific schemata. That his works would receive such wide acclaim and set the stage for a series of emulations of the Chinese Communists' experience in insurgency was perhaps foreseen by Mao because, in his pamphlet *Yu Chi Chan,* written in 1937, he declares:

Historical experience is written in iron and blood. We must point out that the guerrilla campaigns being waged in China today are a page in history that has no precedent. Their influence will not be confined solely to China in her present anti-Japanese war but will be world-wide.[36]

The Contributions of Vo Nguyen Giap

General Giap, presently Minister of Defense in the Communist government of the Democratic Republic of Vietnam, was the military Commander-in-Chief of the Vietminh insurgency forces which fought against the French Army in post-World War II Indochina (1946–1954).

General Giap's principal contributions to Communist theory on insurgency warfare began with his writing of *La Guerre de la Liberation et l'Armée Populaire* (The War of Liberation and the Popular Army) in 1950. This was followed, subsequent to the fall of Dien Bien Phu, by a series of articles about the Vietminh insurgency. They have recently been published in book form under the title *People's War, People's Army.* Excerpts from General Giap's works strikingly illuminate his extensive indebtedness to Mao Tse-tung.

The Vietnamese people's war . . . had to be hard and long lasting in order to succeed in creating conditions for victory. Conceptions born of impatience and aimed at obtaining speedy victory could only be gross errors. It was necessary to accumulate thousands of small victories and to turn them into one great success, gradually altering the balance of forces, transforming our weakness into power, and carrying off final victory.

We contented ourselves with attacking when success was certain, refusing to give battle likely to incur losses to us, or to engage in hazardous actions. In the Vietnamese theater of operations, this method carried off great victories. It could be used in the mountains as well as as in the delta; it could be waged with good or mediocre materiel, even without arms, and was to enable us eventually to equip ourselves at the cost of the enemy.

The Vietnamese war brought out the importance of building resistance bases in the countryside and emphasized the close indissoluble relationship between the anti-imperialist revolution and the antifeudal revolution.

The Vietnamese fighter has always taken care to observe Point 9 of his Oath of Honor: "In contacts with the people, to follow these three recommendations: to respect the people; to help the people; to defend the people . . . in order to win their confidence and affection and achieve a perfect understanding between the people and the army."

Our army has always organized days of help for peasants in production work and in the struggle against flood and drought. It has always observed a correct attitude in its relations with the people. It has never done injury to their property—not even a needle or a bit of thread.

The war of liberation proved that, in the face of an enemy as powerful as he is cruel, victory is possible only by uniting the whole people under a firm and wide natural front based on the worker-peasant alliance.

The strategy of long-term war and the principle of expansion from guerrilla to regular war were successful. . . . Such were the basic strategy and tactics of the people's war in a small and backward agricultural country under the leadership of our Party.[37]

Despite the extensive similarities in content between Mao's writings and the more recent works of General Giap, it would be a mistake to dismiss arbitrarily the latter's parroting as insignificant. It must be remembered that Mao's military opposition was not of the same caliber as Giap's. While Mao did have stiff but sporadic engagements with a modern Japanese military establishment, his greatest victories came after 1945 against the poorly organized and highly demoralized armies of the Kuomintang. General Giap, on the other hand, faced an efficient, modern, and highly professional French army which did not suffer serious morale problems until the seventh year of the eight-year conflict. Hence Giap's experiences with Mao's principles serve as a most significant corroborative exercise.

It must also be noted that the North Vietnamese leader has made a few significant modifications of Mao's theories. For example, although he reiterates Mao's prescriptions that the guerrilla forces befriend the populace at all possible costs, Giap frequently repeats Mao's somewhat muted theme of selective terror, thus elevating this principle to a level higher than that given it by its originator.[38] Giap also modifies the three-stage insurgency theory of his Chinese "mentor" in his *La Guerre de la Libération et l'Armée Populaire.*

While Giap obviously accepts this three-stage theory, he was apparently troubled by his inability to discern clear lines of demarcation between the different stages. One analyst of Southeast Asian affairs has suggested that this problem stemmed from the unique situation in Indochina at the time of this writing (1950). Actually there were two distinct theaters of operation in Vietnam in 1950. The northern theater, Tonkin Delta, was marked by advanced stage operations while the southern theater, Mekong Delta, was characterized by early stage operations. Local conditions dictated this distinction in the modes and scope of conflict in these two areas. The problem of progressive evolution from stage to stage was somewhat more complicated than Giap thought should have been the case after his initial reading of Mao's works on insurgency warfare.

Giap expands Mao's theory of revolutionary stages as it is explicitly concerned with the transition from the second to the third stages. He establishes three preconditions for entry into the last stage: superiority of revolutionary forces, a favorable world situation, and a noticeable weakening of the enemy's resolve. Repeating some of the preconditions in another form, General Giap elaborates on Mao's third stage even further by specifying four subphases within that stage itself: (1) gaining absolute moral superiority over the enemy (that is, achieving full support of the populace for the insurgency cause); (2) regularization and modernization of the army; (3) the occurrence of an international situation that tends to weaken the enemy or directly aid the Communist insurgency; and

(4) the gaining of a momentum that expresses itself in stronger and more purposeful direction of the war effort by the Communist leadership with a corresponding decrease in positive command and control by the enemy.[39]

In his two elaborative amendments to Mao's thoughts on the transition from the second to the third stage, Giap obviously emphasizes the importance of the international political scene upon the conduct of insurgency war. It is this author's contention that Giap's greatest contribution to the body of Communist insurgency warfare theory is precisely this relating of macrocosmic politics to microcosmic internal war.

The Contributions of Ernesto "Che" Guevara

Like the writings of the Vietnamese General Vo Nguyen Giap, those of Major Guevara, a leader of the Cuban revolution against the Batista regime, are essentially a "copy" of Mao Tse-tung's works on insurgency warfare. However, in the more pragmatic and technical aspects of Guevara's work, *La Guerra de Guerrillas*, there is a hint of the influence of General Alberto Bayo, a veteran of guerrilla operations in the Spanish Civil War and a professional left-wing revolutionary. In amalgamating these two influences, the extremely prominent and sophisticated principles of Mao are often "tarnished" by the far less sophisticated Bayo-Guevara elaborations or additions. For example, Major Guevara moves rapidly but clumsily from a general Leninist-Maoist strategic postulate such as:

War is subject to a definite system of scientific laws. Anyone violating them will meet defeat. Guerrilla warfare is governed by the same laws but is also subject to special laws that derive from the particular geographic and social conditions in each country.[40]

to more precise mundane items:

The prerequisites of cleanliness are a piece of soap which will serve for washing of belongings as well as for personal cleanliness, and toothbrush and paste. It is also advisable to carry some books which can be exchanged among other members of the force. The books should be good biographies of heroes of the past, histories or economic geographies (preferably about the country), and some general works which will tend to raise the cultural level of the soldiers.

Very important in the life of a fighter are cigars, cigarettes, or pipe tobacco, for the smoke that can be enjoyed during moments of rest is a great boon to the solitary soldier. A pipe is best, for it allows the fullest use, in times of shortages, of the tobacco of cigarettes and cigar butts.[41]

Yet it may be that the very penchant for elaboration down to the most minute detail will be a strength of this book as it pertains to the spread of Communist insurgency warfare theory to the poorly educated and disenchanted masses of Latin America.

Like Giap's work and despite the obvious heavy indebtedness to Mao, Guevara's book, *La Guerra de Guerrillas*, does contain some positive contributions to Communist theory on insurgency warfare. Guevara's work as it describes the Cuban revolution serves as a corroborative exercise for Maoist principles of action in an Occidental-American environment. It adds to the universality of the prescriptions of the Chinese Communist theorist, and, since the Cuban revolution was successful, it tends to strengthen the *mystique* that has grown up around this particular body of Communist theory on conflict. In addition, Guevara has added a few significant substantive elaborations to this body of theory. At the very beginning of his book, Guevara states:

The Cuban Revolution made three fundamental contributions to the mechanics of revolutionary movements in America:

1. The forces of the people can win a war against the army.
2. It is not necessary to wait for the fulfillment of all conditions for a revolution because the focus of insurrection can create them.
3. The area for the armed struggle in underdeveloped America is the rural regions.[42]

The second conclusion requires additional scrutiny. Guevara makes it quite clear that insurgency leaders who wait for a fortuitous mixture of necessary preconditions for insurgency action are in effect abdicating their "sacred" responsibility. He makes a strong case for catalyzing existing popular grievances so that they will reach the necessary threshold required for positive popular action. In making this point, Guevara leaves no doubt as to the heavy Communist orientation of his philosophy, despite the fact that in the book itself he fails to acknowledge directly this affiliation. Guevara obviously follows the Marxist theory of the inevitability of sociopolitical transformation, and he holds to the Leninist-Maoist prescription of the "Party" as the expediter of the inevitable.

As for the catalyst itself, Guevara blatantly states, "Given suitable operating terrain, land hunger, enemy injustices, etc., a hard core of thirty to fifty men is, in my opinion, enough to initiate armed revolution in any Latin American country."[43] Somewhat related are Guevara's differences with Mao and hence his additions to the body of Communist insurgency theory as they concern the initiation of insurgency and base areas.

Mao does not devote much attention to a discussion of the fundamental initiatory subphases of Stage One in a developing insurgency. Although he does note his initial failures in attempting sustained insurgency via urban uprisings, he skips rather abruptly to guerrilla operations in the rural areas in his coverage of the first stage. The reason is simple: Mao never had to face the problem of organizing guerrilla bands from scratch at the grass-roots level. Instead he organized existing Communist outcasts, disloyal national guardsmen, underpaid private constabularies, and opportunistic bands into guerrilla units. Later he combined these guerrilla forces with Chu Teh's regular army, and the mass for Mao's Communist insurgency military force was thus acquired.[44]

Castro, Guevara, and their eleven cadre men, on the other hand, were forced to form guerrilla insurgency units by drawing upon recruitment sources at the grass-roots level. They had to start essentially from nothing and build a revolutionary force to achieve victory. It is reasonable, therefore, for Guevara to discuss in detail the initiatory steps in creating a viable guerrilla force. Of priority is the assembly of revolutionary leaders and cadre guerrilla fighters in exile or in some isolated spot within an object country "around some respected leader fighting for the salvation of his people."[45] Guevara then calls for elaborate advanced planning, for the advanced establishment of intelligence networks and arsenals, and above all for the continued maintenance of absolute secrecy about the potential insurgency until overt resistance is actually initiated. Thus Guevara fills in the details, overlooked by Mao and only slightly covered by Giap, of the initiatory phases of the first general stage of Maoist insurgency warfare. Notice, however, that Guevara seems far less concerned with the actual stages of insurgency than Giap or Mao, although he accepts without qualification the necessity for moving from guerrilla war to conventional war for final victory.

Concerning base areas, Guevara is more rigid than Mao or Giap. The latter two military theorists and tacticians, while they have extremely high regard for "permanent" base areas, advocate a popular base that can "absorb" the guerrillas after an engagement. Guevara, also relying heavily upon a popular mass base for logistic support and intelligence, does not similarly prescribe periodic absorption of his guerrilla units into the populace. Instead, after an engagement, they are to return to their permanent base in the mountains for regroupment, training, resupply, and rest prior to another strike.

Guevara outdoes Mao in regard to guerrilla war industry. Mao's constantly shifting bases during his Stage One and Two operations hampered his establishment of such quartermaster manufacturing installations despite the fact that Mao fully appreciated their importance and desired their creation. Like Mao, but unlike Giap, Guevara had no foreign sanctuary during the Cuban revolution. Unlike Mao, however, Guevara had the "luxury" of an impenetrable strategic permanent base area in the Sierra Maestra. For Guevara the establishment of rebel war industry (from small arms to shoes to cigars) is both necessary and possible. His writings, therefore, reflect this experience in his many prescriptions concerning the establishment of such industry.

Finally, Guevara has paid far more attention to the importance of urban sabotage units to a guerrilla movement than have his "mentor" Mao or his "colleague" Giap. The Cuban rebel leader specifies in great detail the organization, equipment, and missions of urban sabotage units. He emphasizes the operational concept of complete subordination of the urban units to the general headquarters of the rurally based guerrilla movement:

> It must be pointed out that a suburban guerrilla force cannot be formed by its own efforts. It can be formed only after the creation of certain conditions necessary for its existence. This indicates that a suburban guerrilla force will be directly under the orders of leaders located in other areas. Therefore, such a force does not carry out independent actions, except in accordance with previously established strategic plans. The action must support activities of larger groups located in another area. This is a smaller scale of operations than used by other types of guerrilla forces but it will definitely contribute to the success of some particular tactical objectives. A suburban guerrilla force will not be able to choose between sabotage of telephone services, or other forms of sabotage, or surprising a patrol of soldiers on a distant road— it will do exactly what it is told to do.
>
> The numerical strength of such a force should not exceed four or five men. Limitation to this number is important because the suburban guerrilla force must be regarded as acting in an area that is exceptionally unfavorable; the vigilance of the enemy is much greater and the possibilities of reprisals and of betrayals increase enormously.[46]

In concluding his section on "Suburban Areas," Guevara appears to lecture future students of insurgency warfare on the importance of urban area operations.

> There has been lack of appreciation of the value of guerrilla fighting in the suburbs, but it is, in fact, very important. Appropriate operations of this kind, extended over a wide area, can almost completely paralyze the commercial and industrial life of the area and cause disturbance and distress to the entire population. This makes the people anxious for violent developments to bring an end to their troubles. If thought is given at the beginning

of the war to future possibilities, specialists can be organized for suburban fighting. Then action can be carried out much more rapidly and with a saving for the nation in lives and precious time.[47]

Major Guevara, like Mao Tse-tung, crowns his work with a prophecy of its future impact upon areas outside of the regions of its immediate origin.

The Armed Victory of the Cuban people over the Batista dictatorship has been recognized throughout the world as an epic triumph. It has revised old dogmas about the behavior of Latin American masses and has proved the people's ability to free themselves from an oppressive government through guerrilla warfare.[48]

The pillars of colonialism are crumbling in the face of national and popular struggles in Asia and Africa. The people are united not by religion, race, custom, or hunger, but by common economic and social goals and by a common desire to improve their lot. Asia and Africa joined in Bandung. Now Cuba is uniting Asia and Africa with colonial America.[49]

In a speech in Moscow during the year of publication of *La Guerra de Guerrillas*, Major Guevara leaves no doubt as to the Communist orientation of his prescriptions for insurgency warfare when he declares: "Cuba stands ready to fulfill her Communist-designated goal as a model for armed revolution in Latin America."[50]

This author believes that Major Guevara's principal contributions to Communist insurgency warfare theory are his expositions and postulations of the nature of the initiatory phase of insurgency warfare and, most important, his addition of the urban dimension to guerrilla warfare. This latter point has particularly dangerous implications in Latin America, where most cities are plagued by masses of unemployed. The potential dangers in the marriage of the discontented rural peasants with the discontented newly urbanized and unemployed former peasants through a revolutionary ideology are overwhelming.

In this chapter insurgency warfare was placed in its proper historical perspective, and an outline of the principal theoretical postulations of Communist writers on the subject was presented. It can readily be seen that Soviet contributions to current Communist theory on insurgency warfare seem generally irrelevant. The notable exception is Lenin's general principles concerning the adaptability of the modes of conflict to their respective historical eras and his embryonic concept of protracted war. Soviet utilization of guerrilla warfare tactics has been essentially supplementary to the actions of regular armies and has been defensive and "national" rather than offensive and "class" in character.[51]

The philosophical core of Communist theory of insurgency warfare, as first proclaimed by Mao Tse-tung and then revised slightly by Vo Nguyen Giap and Ernesto Guevara, is the concept of finding weakness in strength and strength in weakness. The fundamental strategic prescription stemming from this concept is the complete politicization of insurgency warfare via the ideological mobilization of the masses in support of the insurgency.

Mao Tse-tung has been described here as being as much a modifier of previous theory as an originator of new theory, but it must be appreciated that his amalgam of the old, the revised, and the original forms the basis for Communist insurgency warfare as it has been practiced in the past three decades. It can be safely assumed that his writings on this subject will continue dramatically to influence the conduct of such warfare in the decades of the 1960's and 1970's.

Finally, it appears that the most significant additions to this body of theory to be made in the post-World War II period are Giap's international dimension and Guevara's urban dimension as a subordinate operational element of the rurally dominated guerrilla effort.

It should be obvious to the reader that insurgency warfare and guerrilla operations are not new designs of international Communism to meet the requirements of the nuclear space age. Rather, they are adaptations of traditional principles of irregular warfare, traditions that have been adopted because of pragmatic necessity and have been wedded to the political-ideological prescriptions of Marxist-Leninist dogma. It is important to appreciate this fact in order better to understand the phenomenon so that the *mystique* which seems to surround this particular body of Communist theory can be dispelled.

4

A Synthesis of Communist Theory and Practice: A Theory of Cellular Development

Now that we have investigated Communist insurgency warfare in its Cold War and historical perspectives, we can achieve further insight by determining current Communist doctrinal prescriptions and by describing this phenomenon analytically. This is achieved by constructing a model of this conflict. This model will be the amalgam of the interaction of relevant published Communist theory with the recorded history of Communist practice in the post-World War II period. This chapter will try to give form to the skeletal framework of the evolved theory presented earlier.

The resultant construct was introduced superficially to the reader when *insurgency* was defined. This definition, in elaborated form, constitutes the central thesis of this chapter. Communist insurgency warfare can be viewed as a cellular development that normally proceeds through the phases of infiltration-subversion, overt armed resistance by small bands, insurrection by large-scale units using guerrilla tactics, and, finally, fruition via civil war.

Before discussing Communist insurgency *per se*, it would

be wise to review briefly the fundamental nature of revolution. It is the contention of many scholars, among them the late N. J. Spykman, that nation-states are able to maintain their unity and structure through a combination of coercion, personal loyalty to leaders, habit, and the acceptance of a common social philosophy, a social myth. This last factor explains and justifies the existing social order in terms of accepted values, and it then projects a social ideal. As long as a national social system permits adequate satisfaction of perceived future needs through its institutions and practices, it will remain stable. When perceived needs and desires are repressed, the social system becomes unstable and ready for revolution.[1]

Apparently accepting this or a similar explanation of revolution, Communist planners of insurgency are immediately confronted with two important assets as they examine the possibilities for this mode of conflict in most of the developing states. First, local perceptions of needs and desires far exceed the capabilities of the indigenous incumbent regimes to meet them. Also, the national social systems themselves tend to inhibit their being met at all. Second, the bonds of nationalism and the acceptance of a generalized social myth within these states are for the most part tenuous.

In countries where these circumstances seem exceptionally promising, Communist planners can prescribe insurgency operations if the Cold War and the strategic deterrence situations favor such action. Indigenous Communist elements then try to harness these assets and seek a detachment of the general populace from its government and even from its traditional way of life. Once this is achieved, the Communists attempt to replace the incumbent regime with a government of their own making. Then they seek the substitution of a Marxist-Leninist order (sometimes modified to permit the practice of religion) for the existing social system. Thus detachment and replacement can be viewed as the two general sequential objectives of Communist insurgency warfare. Detachment is the exclusive objective of the first two phases;

replacement is the principal, but not exclusive, objective of the last two phases.

Phase One: Infiltration-Subversion

Communists put much patient, long, and hard work into preparing the battlefield for insurgency warfare. They normally have many resources in place before they field a guerrilla force and move into second-phase operations. The initial preparation is usually characterized by infiltration of foreign Communist elements into a target state.

The initial tactical objective then becomes the acquisition of local leadership to guide an insurgency through Phase One and into the more advanced and demanding later phases. Foreign and native Communists in an underdeveloped state seek out the politically active voices of dissidence who are found among the indigenous intelligentsia. They then attempt to convince them by academic arguments of the compatibility of Communist doctrine with their nation's "true" aspirations.

An example of this initiatory action in Phase One was the entry of a very small band of Communist agents into Indochina in the 1920's. These Communists joined a labor force assembled in Singapore by French plantation owners to build a railroad in Central Vietnam. They recruited local Vietnamese cadres who were later sent to Paris and Moscow for higher Communist training in insurgency warfare and then returned to lead the Vietnamese against the Japanese in the 1940's and the French in the 1950's.

Communist infiltration into the Philippines began about this same time. The first agents were Malay-Chinese who were later assisted by funds and with personnel from the American Communist Party. The Americans primarily were merchant seamen who established cells in their ports of call. Other examples can be found in the histories of most of the colonial and quasi-colonial areas subsequent to the order to action that emanated from the Second World Congress of the Communist International in 1920.

Prior to World War II, the introduction of Communism into areas with a high insurgency potential was usually accomplished by covert agent infiltration. Since the end of World War II, this function has generally been carried out by the overt activities of Soviet and Chinese Communist embassies, trade missions, and press services as well as by the more traditional activities of covert elements.

It is of interest that the propaganda emanating from Communist-state embassies during Phase One deals with native nationalism and demands for social reform. Upon careful analysis, we find that this propaganda is not the popularly conceived appeal to the masses. Instead, it is an identification of Communism with the sharply oriented sociopolitical outlook of the native intelligentsia.[2] Specific targets for this psychological warfare activity are the disenchanted or unemployed intellectuals.

Once potential insurgency leaders are recruited, they are organized into cells. In these small units, the "recruits" are given a variety of training by the same foreign Communists who recruited them. Outstanding students are then selected for advanced studies in the international seats of Communism —Moscow or Peiping.

A sociological clue to the nature of the initiatory aspects of Phase One Communist insurgency can be found in a largely unnoticed paragraph of the proclamation of the Sixth Comintern Congress of 1928:

. . . experience has shown that, in the majority of colonial and semi-colonial countries, an important if not a predominant part of the Party ranks in the first stage of the movement is recruited from the petty bourgeoisie, and in particular, from the revolutionary inclined intelligentsia, very frequently students. It not uncommonly happens that these elements enter the Party because they see in it the most decisive enemy of imperialism, at the same time not sufficiently understanding that the Communist Party is not only the Party of struggle against imperialist exploita-

tion . . . but struggle against all kinds of exploitation and expro-
priation. Many of these adherents of the Party, in the course of
the revolutionary struggle will reach a proletarian class point of
view.[3]

These newly trained Communist leaders, who generally do
not initially advertise or even admit their Communist affiliation, then begin a two-pronged, subtle psychological offensive
of subversion. This activity is directed at the peasantry (and
perhaps the urban slum dwellers who only recently departed
their pastoral birthplaces) and at the intellectual community
at large. Thus this small detached core of native Communists
seeks further to detach the masses from the government in
order to give a quantitative base to its movement. It also seeks
to detach additional intellectuals to shore up its leadership
cadres or at least to render them sympathetic even though
passive.

This psychological subversion has as its initial target the
minds of men and not the territory of their residence. As it
pertains to the peasant masses, the technique which may be
described as the "for-against-for" is used. Harnessing the rising expectations of the people, the Communists present themselves as being *for* changes that will bring about a satiation of
these expectations. Then they begin their follow-up campaign,
which is directed *against* internal conditions—arbitrary or
corrupt government, inefficient administration, the immorality
of the government leaders, the illegality of the government
itself, high taxes, feudalism—or against foreigners, foreign
ownership, and foreign intervention. The latter assumes special importance in Phase One when such conflict is directly
tied to a struggle for independence. There generally is no
promotion of a specific ideology, except perhaps nationalism;
instead, the emphasis remains negative in nature. The object
is to discredit the incumbent government and the existing
social system.

The final subtle psychological campaign is a return to the
for emphasis, but this time its scope is enlarged. The stand for

change and against the incumbents is combined with a positive offer of a solution to existing problems. The insurgency leaders stand for a reform program, again, generally not yet identified officially with Communist dogma. They propose an alternate social myth or make more basic appeals by manipulating such simple symbols as land and food.[4]

Through the for-against-for technique, the Communist cadres are able to crystallize discontent. Through the harnessing of nationalism, the promotion of an explicit reform program, and the advancement of a palatable substitute social myth, they are able to start organizing the people who share this discontent. It is through organization that the transfer of allegiance from the incumbents to the proponents of change achieves its first real political substance.

As it pertains to the crystallization of the discontented intellectuals, heavy emphasis is placed on nationalism and a rejection of the sociopolitical legacies of colonialism. Character assassination and other techniques of psychological warfare are used to discredit individuals in power. The process of organizing this element ranges from the Communist-cadre elements' covert sponsoring of parties in opposition to the party of the incumbent government to the actual enlistment of government officials to serve secretly the revolutionary movement.

Organization of the masses and the intellectuals usually calls for both the creation of front organizations and the expansion of the covert organization. The latter will ultimately be developed into the militant arm of the insurgency movement. Sometimes, as was the case in Malaya, a Communist party may be legally established concurrently with these covert drives to set up front organizations and to maintain an ever expanding underground establishment.[5] These organizations enable the Communist-cadre elements to control those segments of the populace which have been psychologically detached from the existing sociopolitical system.

It should be noted in passing that the front organizations

created in the 1930's and early 1940's in the Philippines, Malaya, Indochina, and Greece gained a significant advantage from World War II. These organizations, dominated by Communist leaders, became active fighters of the Axis occupation forces. After the war they retained the glamour of military resistance units and therefore commanded much respect from the populace. For example, the HUKS (an abbreviation of the Tagalog term for People's Anti-Japanese Army) represented this type of front organization in the Philippines. The MPAJA (Anti-Japanese People's Army) in Malaya, the National Salvation Units in Vietnam, and the ELAS (National People's Liberation Army) in Greece all were similar front organizations which, politically speaking, profited from the advent of the Second World War. Once these organizations resumed their psychologico-political conflict with the newly reinstalled imperialist regimes or with conservative indigenous governments, the credence of their propaganda attacks was given high value by the masses. Those insurgency movements that were aided by World War II have, with the exception of the present Vietcong insurgency in South Vietnam, blossomed and succeeded (for example, North Vietnam and Yugoslavia) or blossomed only to be defeated (Greece, Malaya, and the Philippines). Future Communist insurgencies in Africa and Latin America will not have the fortuitous legacy of a similar major war. Hence their preparations for insurgency will follow more closely the patterns of development described here.

After the establishment of front organizations, and perhaps in some cases even after the emergence of an overt Communist party, infiltration and subversion continue at an accelerated pace. The scope for crystallization and organization activities is expanded, and the incumbent regime is forced to respond to this threat of systematic detachment of the populace that is posed by Phase One Communist insurgency warfare. T. E. Lawrence contended that a successful guerrilla insurgency could be effected if 2 per cent of the populace actively supported the striking forces, provided the remainder was passively sympathetic. Post-World War II insurgencies in developing areas tend to sanctify the correctness of this postulation.

If the government becomes demoralized and fails in its attempts effectively to counter insurgent propaganda, and if it is equally inept in controlling sporadic demonstrations sponsored by front organizations, the insurgency need not pass to the next phase for fruition. The insurgents will win by default. If the incumbent government refuses to capitulate to these pressures, the conflict may well increase in intensity, and an additional mode of warfare will enter the combat ledger. The insurgency will move into Phase Two—overt armed resistance by small guerrilla bands.

Even though the greater part of any Phase One operation is covert and marked by a subtle, gradual deterioration of the existing sociopolitical system, this phase is an extremely important link in the chain of Communist insurgency warfare. The lack of success of the Malayan Communist insurgency and of the first and second Tudeh insurgencies in Iran can be attributed in no small part to dramatic failures in this particular phase of operations. There are strong indications that the war of moral attrition which characterizes this phase is also being experienced by many underdeveloped states in Latin America (for example, Venezuela, Colombia, and Guatemala). It also can be assumed that patient battleground preparations for insurgency warfare are being carried on in the Middle East and in many of the newly emergent states and the remaining colonial possessions of Africa.

Phase Two: Small Band Operations

Communist theory prescribes no time length for the completion of each phase. Mao's concept of "revolutionary flow" is always available as a legitimate rationalization for retreat either from one phase to a preceding phase or from a more overt and direct activity to a more covert and indirect activity within a given phase. Tactically speaking, however, it is conceivable that the "objective conditions" of a given situation may actually force an indigenous insurgency leadership into drafting a timetable and attempting to adhere to it in a rigid fashion.

Faced with the necessity of responding to an incumbent government's repression operations, the indigenous Communist leadership can either retreat to the more passive aspects of Phase One operations or direct the insurgency into Phase Two. Among the most important inputs into the decision-making equation of this leadership at this crucial point are: the condition of the battleground that is initially to support, and then sustain, Phase Two operations; the estimated vitality of the incumbent regime and its capabilities for carrying on Phase One counterinsurgency versus its capability for carrying out Phase Two counterinsurgency operations (including an assessment of the likelihood of external aid for the incumbents); external politico-military factors, such as the Cold War and the strategic nuclear stalemate. The degree of importance assigned to this last-mentioned compound input is directly related to the anticipated degree of material and diplomatic support required by the insurgent forces from the established seats of Communist power.

It will be assumed, for the purpose of continuing the development of this cellular thesis, that the decision is made to move insurgency operations into the second phase. The principal objective of this phase, like that of the preceding one, is the detachment of the populace from the government and from the traditional social system. Phase One activities of infiltration-subversion also continue insofar as they are possible. With the addition of Phase Two operational concepts, however, new devices are employed in breaking the existing bonds between the government and the people.

In Phase One the discontent of the masses and the intelligentsia has been crystallized in certain segments of these

support functions for any guerrilla raids carried out in their local area.

During this phase there is usually no effective organization above the village level. But there often is a small staff at the district level serving as the core for a full military-civil command section during Phase Three. Similarly, there may be regional (or provincial) headquarters cadres at the next highest level[7]; they start filling out and assuming operational significance during the latter periods of the second phase.

During Phase Two there is a lack of unitary control over the various village armed bands. Topographical conditions, the lack of a good road net, and the lack of proper organic communications equipment compound the problems of the Communist leadership in their attempts to coordinate band operations.

The village armed bands usually operate from three distinct bases. The first is the popular base—or general base of opportunity—which consists of supporters among the general populace who provide food and shelter for the guerrillas who also live among the general populace. Second, is the roving or movable base, which is nothing more than the frequent shifting of camp sites in areas difficult to traverse. Third, is the isolated mountain, forest, or swamp base which is static and is inaccessible to the incumbent forces, thereby providing the insurgents with a valuable area for rest, recuperation, and training. This base usually is supplied with the necessities of life and intelligence by part-time insurgent personnel living in nearby villages.

If the villagers are unsympathetic to the insurgent movement or if their actions are so carefully guarded by incumbent military forces that it is difficult to collect and dispatch materials to the guerrilla base(s), then the small bands will launch raids on commercial or government supply trains. Or they will occupy a town in the evening and requisition necessary supplies from the farmers or merchants, paying them either in currency or in notes of debt. In some instances the insurgents actually capture large estates owned by absentee landlords and harvest the crops themselves. This was done extensively by the Philippine Communist insurgents in 1951–1952.

The acquisition of arms during Phase Two is normally more difficult than is the procurement of food and clothing. The local native community does not possess this necessary resource. It must therefore be obtained either from the enemy or from friendly outside sources.

In the special cases of the Vietminh, Philippine HUK, Greek ELAS, and Malayan Communist insurgencies, the arms supply problem during Phase Two was solved by the farsighted actions of the anti-Axis, popular front, guerrilla units which were the forerunners of the Communist insurgency organizations. These Communist-controlled World War II organizations hid their arms rather than turn them in after the cessation of hostilities. Hence caches of weapons and ammunition were available to the insurgent forces when they moved into Phase Two operations. These caches, however, were not really sufficient for sustained, long-term Phase Two operations, let alone sufficient to permit a rational decision to move to the succeeding phase without substantial additional outside support.

Most Communist insurgency campaigns in the next two decades will be denied the asset of a World War supply system. Unless bases can be established in areas contiguous to a Communist state, the principal source of arms will have to be internal. The insurgents will be compelled to purchase, steal, or capture weapons from the enemy. (Castro's forces bought arms from corrupt Batista officials.) Ordnance depots and weapons supply convoys can consequently be considered as prime targets for Phase Two military action.

When base areas are adjacent to a Communist state, arms undoubtedly will be received from external sources. The Vietminh, the Vietcong, and the ELAS insurgencies were marked by this type of support.[8] Sometimes static bases may be located in the foreign states themselves. If the object state has a long shore line and an inadequate coastal patrol capability, arms can be shipped in covertly via surface cargo vessels. In particular situations, such as Laos and the Congo, insurgent forces may actually get air-dropped arms supplies from nontiguous Communist allies. This indicates graphically that the threat of sponsored Communist insurrections is pervasive. It may vary in degree due to geographic considerations, but it is never absent if the international and local situations dictate action against a target (nation) of opportunity.

The next important requirement is a continuous source of recruits. Generally, men are more plentiful than weapons during Phase Two. As this phase is extended over a long period, or as it starts to trigger the third phase, the need for greater numbers of troops for combat and support units increases dramatically. Levies are made directly on villages under total or partial insurgent control. Propaganda activities are concentrated on attracting the youth to fight against foreign imperialists or reactionary indigenous puppets. The reward for such service is a promise of first-class citizenship in the new order. Many youngsters join for excitement, others for organizational security. Some enlist for a chance to acquire a social status exceeding the one they possess by virtue of their birth or limited education.[9]

Once these small bands have their weapons and personnel, have established supply and intelligence networks, and have bases from which to operate, this phase will have gone through its own internal processes of crystallization and organization. The initiation of tactical operations is then in order. These military operations constitute the militarization of Phase Two. Of course, in a broader perspective, Phase Two itself, as a composite whole, is the terminal militarization aspect of the general series of crystallization and organization operations that have occurred during the first phase.

In moving through the internal Phase Two aspects of crystallization and organization, the principal tactics used against the general populace are friendly persuasion and terror. Mao Tse-tung and Che Guevara strongly urge all insurgents to follow friendly persuasion. They reject terror almost totally because it is loaded with long-term liabilities even though its employment may bring about tempting short-term benefits.

An important element in the defeats of the Malayan, Philippine, and Greek Communist insurgencies was the fact that terrorist operations against the people backfired. Instead of insuring consolidated support through fear, terrorism engendered antipathy for the insurgents and thus alienated a significant portion of the masses. It is true that the non-Communist FLN's terrorist activities in Algeria against indigenous Arabs did not completely alienate the insurgents and cause the demise of their revolutionary movement. There are two reasons for this: the French also used terror tactics against the Moslems, thus nullifying any psychological advantage that might have accrued to them had they not used such techniques; in any insurgency directed against a foreign element, there is an extra dimension of ethnic solidarity among the insurgents and the masses that causes the latter to forgive such excesses by its brother guerrilla fighters.

The use of general terror tactics against the people often indicates that the insurgents' propaganda activities ("political mobilization") have failed to convince the people voluntarily to support the guerrilla bands. A review of history suggests that the degree of voluntary support from the populace for a particular insurgency begins to wane if the conflict drags on without any demonstrable sign of significant insurgent successes.[10] Thus the use of terror is often a sign of failure and should be viewed as such. The use of terror against officials of the regime, however, is a different matter entirely. Even this type of terror, if it is not selective, can lead to long-term problems for the insurgents.

It should be re-emphasized that the principal objective of Phase Two operations is still the detachment of the populace from the existing sociopolitical system. Specialized terror tactics can be used effectively in two ways. Terror-breeding acts can be directed against key official or quasi-official personnel and certain installations that make up the social and economic institutions of a community. Attacks against schoolteachers, doctors, grain-mill operators, agricultural technicians, and the like are designed to create local socioeconomic chaos which in turn can be harnessed to Communist ends. If the insurgents can quickly capitalize upon this locally induced instability which adds to existing national instability, establish their own control over the area, and then replace these socioeconomic institutions with those of their own design, then this terror can have utility for them. If the insurgents are unable to fill the void created by their destructive acts, then this type of socioeconomic directed terrorism may result in the alienation of a people from the movement. It may in fact turn the people against the insurgency.

Terror can effectively be directed against local political and central government officials, and certain representatives of the established order can be eliminated. Such action generally creates two situations, both of which favor the insurgents. First, the colleagues of the victims of this specialized terrorism (kidnaping and murder) tend to become demoralized, and hence public administration suffers. Second, irreconcilable incumbent leaders or supporters are eliminated, thus removing obstacles to the increase of insurgency control. As Mao Tse-tung pointed out, however, even this type of terror may backfire. It may so enrage a "decaying" civil and military service of an incumbent government that an otherwise ineffective and lethargic regime may be catalyzed into an efficient counterinsurgency force. Castro's guerrillas followed Mao's advice to the extent that they even released all prisoners after they were disarmed, and the 26th of July movement succeeded in defeating the better armed but "morally inferior" Batista forces.[11]

These last two ways of using terror are designed to illuminate the weaknesses of the incumbent regime, to discredit its

power, and to undermine its authority.[12] The most effective
tactic used to secure this objective during Phase Two is not
terrorism *per se*; instead, it is the broader concept of irregular
conflict, guerrilla warfare.

Guerrilla warfare is conducted by civilians who usually
have little formal military experience and little patience with
the tactical prescriptions employed by professional military
establishments. These civilians operate in small bands and
during Phase Two are generally tied, via their bases, to their
villages because supply and communications problems prevent larger groupments. Political indoctrination rather than
traditional unit *esprit* serves as the psychological glue for each
unit. Because mobility is the key to survival for small guerrilla
bands faced by a modern-equipped incumbent army, the arms
of the guerrillas are light and small. The largest weapons
during Phase Two operations are the light machine gun and
the small portable mortar. Nothing that has to be moved by a
wheeled vehicle is of value to the guerrilla. Whereas, among
his conventional regular counterparts, wheels are somewhat
of a synonym for mobility, for the guerrilla they are a symbol
of immobility.[13]

Other characteristics of the guerrilla units include: life for
the individual fighter is extremely harsh; he must live either
without the amenities of civilized life, or, if he lives with them,
he is under constant threat of discovery. Guerrillas are generally denied women and alcohol. They fight knowing that, if
they are wounded, their medical care will be rudimentary at
best and that, if they die, few will know where they are buried.

The tactical *modus operandi* of these small bands is captured graphically in the words of Mao Tse-tung quoted in the
preceding chapter. These guerrilla forces conduct war along
exterior lines. They employ offensive tactics that involve a
high degree of surprise, require the fewest men, present the
lowest risk, and provide the greatest chance for limited victory
and quick disengagement. Road ambushes of government
convoys, sabotage of military and economic installations, raid-

ing patrols, and prolonged sieges of selected isolated military outposts with small arms fire constitute typical Phase Two guerrilla activities. These operations in the rural areas normally involve men-to-men engagements between the insurgents and incumbents on a limited scale. The urban insurgents, however, avoid such contacts as they carry out their sabotage or support missions.

Sound intelligence is fundamental to the success of guerrilla attacks. Information on where and when to attack and when to disengage is an imperative need of insurgent unit commanders. A steady supply of intelligence from the part-time village insurgent personnel who are associated with a particular band permits a guerrilla force to gain maximum advantage from its cross-country mobility capability.

All these operations are so directed within a particular guerrilla area as to cause the government's army to disperse its superior forces to meet these numerous small-scale military challenges.

Similar small-scale operations by guerrilla units in other areas compound the general problem for the incumbent government's army. Whether these guerrilla units coordinate their attacks—and they normally do not have the communications and control capability for such coordination during Phase Two —the most plausible solution as viewed by the counterinsurgency commanders is generally more dispersion of forces. Hence limited local concentrations by the insurgent units cause unlimited dispersion of the stronger government forces. It is precisely in this antithetical situation that one can distinguish between the general tactics of guerrilla and conventional warfare.

It is precisely in this way that the small guerrilla bands preclude the incumbent forces from making full use of their material and numerical superiority. Given this situation and the hit-and-run tactics of these bands, the insurgent forces easily gain a reputation for invincibility. At the same time, the regular forces of the government's army gain the reputation of being inept, bumbling fools. The incumbent government itself is reflected in this adverse light. The populace sees it as being unable to provide security for the people. Thus Phase Two operations contribute greatly to the achievement of the objective initially advanced in the first phase—detachment of the people from the incumbent regime. With the possible exception of the Indonesian and Tunisian non-Communist revolutions, very few insurgencies have been successfully terminated through the utilization of Phase Two alone. In these two cases, international pressure was the decisive factor that forced the Dutch and French respectively to withdraw.

As the insurgency develops, certain fundamental changes occur before Phase Three begins. In addition to launching raiding parties from their village-base complexes, the insurgents begin sending out armed propaganda-team sorties. These specialized guerrilla units begin expanding the area of control for their particular band. They serve as missionaries and convert people in adjacent villages to their cause. They provide the cadres for the development of new guerrilla units and village support forces. Through these activities certain districts become in effect blanketed by insurgent small band forces. Such continuity permits some sort of district organization and unitary control. With the acquisition of some communications equipment, control can be strengthened and made tactically more effective. Similar expansion of a few districts may even permit the establishment of one or two regional command centers.

As this cellular growth within Phase Two progresses—by continued crystallization and organization—military considerations play an increasing role in selecting targets for guerrilla strikes. During the greater part of Phase Two operations, political considerations—"what can be done to insure best the detachment of people and the demoralization of the opposition"—play the dominant role in insurgent military action. As Phase Three approaches, however, it becomes necessary to prepare the battleground for the expanded military operations of insurrection. The political factor is still given high consideration, but the necessity for destroying infrastructure targets —bridges, communications lines, railroads—so that a large area can be isolated from enemy action, becomes most important. For the objective of Phase Three is the complete replacement of incumbent government control over a carefully integrated geographical area.

Phase Three: Insurrection

Phase One and Phase Two operations prepare the psychological battleground for the insurgency by the detachment of a people from the existing sociopolitical system. The principal objective of Phase Three is replacement. The insurgent movement now seeks to fill in, on a substantial scale, the psychological void created by its successes in the preceding phases. It greatly expands its propaganda activities. It provides the people, on a massive scale, with a reformist and nationalistic ideology to replace the partially discredited social myth that has been an important cohesive element within the existing national order. As in Phase Two, the insurgent movement may or may not overtly identify itself as a Communist-directed activity.

Like its biological counterparts, the sociopolitical cells of insurgency become larger and more complex as they move from phase to phase. In Phase Three a substantial area comes under direct overt control of the insurgency movement. This area is usually a regional or provincial subdivision of a particular underdeveloped state. The insurgents fill out the regional organizational machinery, both civil and military, that was established in embryonic form during Phase Two in those areas showing greatest promise of insurgency success. Normally, a particularly strong static base serves as the seed for expansion to a regional area for Phase Three operations. These key bases may or may not be contiguous to friendly Communist states. In Greece, during the ELAS insurgency, small bases in the Grammos Mountains (on the frontier with Albania), the Vitsi Mountains (on the frontier with Yugoslavia), and the Pende Mountains (in the central part of the country) developed through Phase Two into substantial Phase Three, regional, insurgency areas. In the Philippines the small Phase Two HUK redoubt on Mt. Arayat was similarly expanded to include a sizable area in Central Luzon, and in Cuba the two or three small bases in the Sierra Maestra Mountains were expanded to include a substantial amount of Oriente province as these two insurgencies respectively emerged into Phase Three. In Laos small, separated Phase Two bases were consolidated within the provinces of Sam Neua and Phone Saly and brought under a centralized control as the Pathet Lao insurgency moved into the insurrection stage in the late 1950's.

The organizational structure within a Phase Three regional base resembles the bureaucratic establishment of comparable provinces within the affected state. There are some outstanding differences; for example, political officers of the guerrilla force hold all positions which would normally be considered civil assignments. Important bureaus such as intelligence, logistics, and personnel procurement are attached to the standard governmental structure. These agencies, as their titles suggest, have military support missions to perform.

Although its primary purpose is to support the military, the intelligence organization is civilian based in virtually all respects. The network runs from the rural hamlets to minor officials and functionaries at provincial and central government levels.

The logistics establishment has activities ranging from the procurement of basic war materials and foodstuffs from the general populace, to the establishment of guerrilla industries and guerrilla farm plots, to the procurement of sophisticated war material from external sources. Complex overt-covert supply networks that extend beyond the secured insurgency area are created, using animal-pack trails and domiciliary way stations. Guerrilla goods are stored here during the day and are moved along the trails under cover of darkness (to prevent air interdiction) by part-time insurgents who live in the bordering villages.

The delivery of supplies from contiguous or not too distant Communist states becomes considerably easier and entails less risks to the deliverers once third-phase base areas are established. Drop sites (and surface debarkation sites) are prepared and elaborately concealed trails from a contiguous Communist state to the insurgent area are developed. An example of air-drop support to a third-phase insurgency was the more than one hundred sorties flown by Soviet aircraft in supplying material to the Pathet Lao forces in early 1961. Numerous North Vietnamese specialists also were parachuted into the insurgent area to provide the expertise necessary for expanded operations. It is not unusual for an insurgent force to begin receiving covert military advisory assistance from bloc nations once a third-phase base area appears secure.

Besides the rapid stockpiling of material, much emphasis is placed on recruiting more full-time guerrillas, on the establishment of an extensive reserve system, and on the creation and training of regular army units. This necessity arises not only out of the anticipated needs preparatory to the initiation of full-scale civil war, Phase Four. If voluntary recruitments run below estimated needs in personnel, this phase is often marked by forced abductions. This last resort measure, like the use of terror, is risky. Greek ELAS insurgents, for example, used forced abductions extensively during their Phase Three buildup. These inductees, however, proved to be poor fighters and often became intelligence agents for the Greek National Army. Therefore, voluntary enlistments, as Mao prescribes, must, if at all possible, be the exclusive means of filling out the units. Insurgent propaganda during this phase will be focused on inducements to the general populace to join the military units of the insurgency. Guerrilla raids, no matter how modest their achievements, will be advertised as great military successes. Victory will be portrayed as imminent.

The general military organization during this phase consists of three operational levels: regional, district, and local (villages). Troops assigned to the regional units, perhaps two or three battalions, are the best-trained and best-armed personnel within the movement. They form the mobile columns or strike forces that are the backbone of the insurgent's military establishment. At the next lower level there is generally one battalion per district. Such a district battalion is made up of full-time guerrilla cadres and part-time troops in each subordinate company. The village level is also composed of both full-time and part-time guerrillas with the latter numerically predominant.

Through the acquisition of radios from external sources, or possibly by capture, this three-level organization is joined into a composite operational entity. Unlike Phase Two, the movements of units at all three levels are controlled by a central headquarters; each unit's actions are coordinated with the actions of other units in the achievement of common military and political goals.

Despite the fact that a Phase Three base area is considered secure by the insurgents so that both civil and military administrative machinery functions continually, the insurgent armed forces of this area will not normally elect to fight positional battles—even to defend key installations within the area itself. By the time Phase Three has evolved, however, the incumbent government's forces either have consolidated in a defensive configuration of forts located at strategically important points or have abandoned the hostile countryside for the security of the larger urban centers. Guerrilla commanders are not ordinarily confronted with the choice of staying to defend or retreating from a key installation within the secured area. However, the temptation to stay and defend is much greater in Phase Three than in Phase Two. History shows that the Greek ELAS insurgents succumbed to this temptation and were decisively defeated. General Giap, profiting from a similar earlier mistake, did not succumb to this temptation in the 1953–1954 campaigns of the Vietminh, so this insurgency went into Phase Four and victory at Dien Bien Phu.

A typical strike operation during this phase finds a regional unit moving out of its redoubt area toward its target. Along the way it will pick up district and village units so that, by the time it arrives at its destination, the original force has been perhaps tripled. This augmented force strikes, carries out its mission, and returns to the base area. During the skirmish and the withdrawal, part-time insurgents provide covering support for the strike force and supply it with timely intelligence.

Phase Three military actions are really no more than large-scale, well-coordinated guerrilla operations that are launched from large, secure base areas. In addition to the military strikes that are increasingly aimed at acquiring additional supplies and isolating an ever expanding area from incumbent control, armed propaganda sorties are carried out in the enemy's rear. The psychological warfare teams have as their objective the further undermining of the authority of the government and the recruitment and organization of additional insurgent units. Strong efforts are made to conquer and create additional regional-size secure areas before the insurgency moves into the fourth stage.

The most noticeable characteristic of Phase Three is the high pitch of activity both in the acquisition of the means of warfare and in the increase in the number and scope of military operations themselves. Also noticeable will be personnel changes at command levels. As the needs occur for filling district or regional staff and command positions, the more successful small band commanders are normally promoted. These officers, however, often do not possess the managerial expertise and military sophistication needed for high-level operations. Demotions, replacements by former subordinates, and other unstabilizing personnel problems may develop during the Phase Three period. Such was the case in the Communist HUK insurgency in the Philippines and the non-Communist FLN insurgency in Algeria.

The creation, or perhaps the emergence, of a government-in-exile is usually a characteristic of this particular phase. This may be significant in more than a diplomatic sense. For in some cultures men seem hesitant to engage in violence without moral justification. By the creation of a government-in-exile, violence against the incumbent regime can be interpreted by some morally restrained potential insurgents as now being legal. In short, such a government can serve as a formal source of moral dispensation for acts against the incumbent regime.[14]

Finally, another characteristic of Phase Three, especially as it pertains to its terminal period, is that military considerations begin to get as much attention as political considerations in target selections for the strike forces. As the beginning of civil war approaches, it becomes more and more imperative that the physical battlefield be so prepared as to facilitate the transition from guerrilla warfare to conventional warfare.

Phase Four: Civil War

Little space will be devoted to this particular phase because its characteristics closely approach those of conventional limited war, which is extensively covered in existing military literature.

The decision to move into Phase Four operations is determined to a significant extent by conditions in the external Cold War situation. Unless the incumbent regime has almost completely collapsed from within, there is a real probability that Phase Four may be extended to such a point that substantial externally supplied aid will be necessary to insure victory for the insurgents. Close consultation with one or more of the major Communist powers will be a prerequisite for such a decision.

Even though mobility is still an important aspect of Phase Four operations by regularized guerrillas or a newly created regular insurgent army and small guerrilla bands still operate in ancillary roles, the fundamental nature of the military conflict changes in this period. Viewed within the four-phased context of Communist insurgency warfare, the most striking military features of the fourth phase are the dominance of conventional organization concepts and conventional operational tactics.

The objective of this phase, too, is replacement, except that the replacement objective here is total in nature. It represents the fulfillment of the insurgency itself, the substitution of a government created by the insurgents for the discredited and defeated incumbent regime.

By the time Phase Four begins, the objective of the first two phases, detachment, which has been continually pursued in an ever expanding fashion, begins to bear the heavy fruit of full achievement. The masses, psychologically detached from the existing government, either join the insurgents directly, support them, or sit and wait passively for the beginning of the new order which promises dramatic beneficial changes.

The incumbent's army, demoralized by defeats and by the antipathy or apathy of the general populace, proves to be no match for the newly created conventional insurgent army. The equipment and training of the incumbent government's forces are still vastly superior to that of the insurgent forces, but the will to fight and the cause for dying have slowly disappeared. Thus a victory for Communism occurs through a carefully planned and executed strategy of the cellular development of insurgency in an underdeveloped area.

If we use this model of cellular development as a frame of reference, we will note that the most dramatic Communist successes occurred where the insurgency had completed a full four-stage development—China, North Vietnam, and Cuba. On the other hand, the significant defeats of Communist insurgency have all occurred before the last phase was entered: the Greek ELAS insurgency as it prematurely went into the fourth phase; the Philippine HUK insurgency in Phase Three; the Iranian Tudeh, the Malayan MRLA, and the Communist-inspired Mau-Mau insurgency in Kenya in Phase Two; the Arbenz-led Guatemalan insurgency in Phase One. The sooner a Communist insurgency can be recognized and the earlier the counterinsurgency operations can begin in earnest, the greater will be the chances of success for the incumbent regime.

The model presented in this chapter can have far greater utility than serving simply as a device for retrospective analysis. By helping to understand this phenomenon of Communist insurgency warfare in a more definitive and comprehensive manner—especially when it is combined with or placed within the framework of the contributory factors of insurgency scheme (as developed in Chapter 2)—this construct can serve as the basis for the systematic design of a counterinsurgency doctrine for the West.

At the time of this writing, no real counterinsurgency doctrine exists either for directly affected emerging states or for the indirectly affected leader-state of the Free World. There are bits and pieces of relevant military and political lore that appear as separate subjects in field manuals, military and political journals, and other government publications. This doctrinal potpourri reflects the "play it by ear" character of the United States and the West's tactics and strategy for actions against Communist insurgency. Much of this pertinent literature contains pleas for a counterinsurgency doctrine. The West must so order and so orient its counterinsurgency endeavors that it can expect favorable and lasting returns for its resource and prestige investments in these important conflict situations.

Part Two of this book will be concerned with the design of just such a general doctrine. Using the above-described model of Communist insurgency as the primary reference object—and recognizing that adjustments may have to be made in it to suit the peculiarities of each distinct geographic and cultural area—the following chapters will contain refutations of certain traditional postulations about counterinsurgency operations and endorsements of others. These chapters will also present original proposals regarding concepts, strategy, and tactics designed to defeat this Communist threat. The resultant amalgam will focus primarily on the employment of military forces—both surface and air, both indigenous and foreign, both in destructive and in constructive roles—to defeat this political, military, and sociopsychological phenomenon at each phase of cellular development. Hopefully, this body of organized prescriptions will help to fill the doctrinal void now besetting the West in its war against Communist insurgency in the emerging areas.

PART TWO

The Incumbent Regime's Response: Counterinsurgency Warfare

5

The Combat Role
of the Military:
Surface Operations

Let us return to the medical analogy introduced earlier. Chapters 2 through 4 can be viewed collectively as a comprehensive diagnostic report of a socio-political-military disease that threatens the underdeveloped states directly and the West indirectly. This disease must be eradicated before it spreads and results in a serious debilitation of the Free World. The problems posed by this threat fall into the three areas of preventive, therapeutic, and regenerative medicine.

The preventive aspects must be carried out through socio-economic-political reform within an infected underdeveloped state. Injections of economic and technological assistance from an external source can permit such a state to both broaden and to accelerate its development programs. The therapeutic aspects call for the isolation of the disease organisms, followed by their destruction or at least their neutralization. This action should be carried out as far as possible by indigenous agencies alone. However, if the necessary capabilities are not present within the local military establishment, supplemental injections of military aid and advisory assist-

ance from an ally will be necessary. The regenerative programs—reconstruction, rehabilitation, and nation-building
—will undoubtedly require an amalgam of both local and
foreign capital and expertise.

This chapter will consider strategic and operational doctrine for military surface actions to meet the therapeutic
requirements in the intermediate stages of insurgency. Because guerrilla warfare is the principal mode of conflict in
these stages, heavy emphasis will be placed on counterguerrilla operations. Chapter 6 will discuss the role of airpower
and organizational prescriptions for counterinsurgency combat operations. Chapter 7 will cover the use of indigenous
armed forces in constructive operations—for the prevention
of Communist insurgency or for the regeneration of developing nations which have successfully defeated Communist
guerrillas in combat operations. No proposed response to
Phase Four Communist insurgency warfare will be presented
because, as noted earlier, conventional, limited war is the
subject of vast numbers of excellent works in military science.

Some Preliminary Conceptual Considerations

It is imperative that counterinsurgency planners consider
operations against insurgents as not falling within the pur-
view of general conventional warfare in which regular infantry, armor, and artillery units employ standard tactics and
organization to defeat the enemy. A good regular infantry
trooper is not automatically an effective counterinsurgent
unless he has received special training. The French learned
this bitter lesson in Indochina. Central government armed
forces will be tempted to make the same tragic mistake unless
they complement their standard conventional units with
Ranger (Commando) troops and modify their general training programs and operational doctrine to reflect the peculiar
nature of the threat posed by insurgent bands. It is equally

imperative that counterinsurgency planners not go completely in the opposite direction and attempt to emulate precisely the organization and tactics of the insurgent bands. This temptation is always present in an insurgency situation. The rationale is that once the better trained, armed, and disciplined troops of the incumbent government master the tactics of the guerrillas, the latter will be no match for them in fire fights; hence, the insurgent forces will be defeated. This reasoning, of course, overlooks the fact that vital support items (such as an extensive intelligence net among the rural populace and great familiarity with local terrain features) may be denied to the incumbent government's forces. Also, this course of action may misleadingly compel these forces to give up voluntarily a particular capability (mobility or fire power, for example), because it was designed for conventional war and does not seem compatible with their new posture and tactics.

Not quite so misleading, but still a matter for some concern, is the acceptance of a similar view by those more industrially advanced states called upon to supply war material and technical advice to an insurgency-troubled ally. Literature on counterinsurgency warfare in the United Kingdom and the United States contains numerous references to the fighting of battles in pre-World War II style. In these states old equipment has been overhauled and placed in the active inventory of special counterguerrilla organizations on the assumption that it was best suited to the particular climatological and topographical features of many high-potential insurgency areas. In general, this is true. But it merely reinforces the fixed idea of an old-type war fought with old-type weapons under old-time tactical concepts modified only by the introduction of a few modern devices such as lightweight small arms and communications equipment and the ubiquitous helicopter.

The probability that such an error could be made by responsible decision-makers seems small because of the obviousness of its consequences. Yet the subtle nostalgic temptation to make such an error is ever present and should be appreciated. Once it is made, certain doors to the creative application of technology to the special problems of insurgency warfare will be closed.

Another conceptual problem concerns the apparent inability of many leaders in the developing states to view Phase Two and Phase Three insurgency warfare as anything but military operations. This is especially acute in Latin America where some conservative elements dominate both military and civilian political hierarchies. This view obviously must be corrected, and the strategy and tactics of counterinsurgency warfare must reflect the marriage of sociopolitical and military considerations. Such a conceptual amalgam recognizes the all-important role of the general populace in deciding the outcome of any insurgency war.

The native population must be taken into account in all counterinsurgency warfare planning, regardless of the level of operations. Any objective and any method of achieving the objective which will alienate the population should be avoided if at all possible. The people must be convinced that they have a common cause with the incumbent government. They must be willing to cooperate to the extent of fighting and dying, if necessary, to protect their villages from the insurgents. If this cooperation between the people and the government does not develop, the counterinsurgency campaign is doomed to eventual failure. This is fundamental.

As psycho-political support accrues to the incumbent regime, it must be converted into the more tangible asset of increases in available manpower for military and police service. The necessity for this conversion is illustrated in the following statistical analyses: (1) in general, one guerrilla is capable of tying down or dissipating the usefulness of ten conventional soldiers; (2) fifteen regular troops are killed for every guerrilla fatality[1]; (3) in Malaya, it required 6,500 hours of patrol or ambush time to see a single Communist guerrilla, and, of those spotted, only one out of ten was killed or captured[2]; (4) also in Malaya, it took at 30:1 ratio of counterinsurgents to guerrillas to effect victory[3]; (5) in Greece, 200,000 regular troops were employed to defeat 30,000 guerrillas[4]; (6) in South Vietnam, during the period 1957–1962, the Phase Two ratio was twenty-five counterinsurgents for each Vietcong guerrilla.[5] These figures illustrate undeniably the importance and necessity of a vast manpower reservoir if the incumbent regime is successfully to pursue counterinsurgency warfare.

The central imperatives of therapy for Phase Two and Phase Three are the establishment and systematic achievement of three general objectives: (1) control over the greatest possible number of people; (2) the weakening and physical exposure of the insurgent guerrilla forces; and (3) the defeat of the guerrilla forces. These objectives are interrelated and must be pursued simultaneously at both the strategic and the tactical levels.

In the remainder of this chapter we shall present a discussion of military surface operations that can be employed to achieve these objectives. This will be followed by prescriptions for the utilization of airpower in case the incumbent regime acquires such aid from an industrially advanced ally. Finally, we shall cover organizational considerations and prescriptions for the efficient coordination of surface and air forces and civil and military organizations in an effective counterinsurgency campaign.

Control of the Populace

The history of past counterinsurgency wars shows that in most cases an incumbent regime has been late in responding to the insurgent threat, and its initial response has generally been too modest to be effective. This mistake will probably be repeated again by many developing states understandably reluctant to commit the extensive resources required to eradicate small insurgent bands. In many areas an insurgency will be well along into Phase Two or perhaps even into Phase Three before the incumbent regime recognizes the gravity of the threat and reacts with determination. It goes without saying that the response at this later stage will be more costly and more disruptive of economic development than a concerted response would have been in an earlier phase.

Once a decision to act is made, the first objective must be the gaining or regaining of control over the bulk of the national population. This will remain an important consideration throughout the counterinsurgency campaign.

Consolidation and Counterattack—The first step in achieving this objective is the nonmilitary psycho-political task of recasting the social myth associated with the incumbent regime so that it will reflect the changed values of the populace as a whole. Second, easily discernible socioeconomic reforms that have an immediate impact must be instituted as evidence of the government's sincerity in alleviating grievances and meeting the rising expectations of the masses. An example of this was President Ngo Dinh Diem's partially successful agricultural credit program, which was designed to free the bulk of the poor peasants from the hands of exploiting usurers.[6]

These reform activities must be effectively advertised by all existing methods. (The term *psychological-action* will embrace all operations directed at friendly or uncommitted personnel. *Psychological-warfare* will refer to operations directed against the enemy. This distinction is similar to the French Army's concepts of *l'action psychologique* and *la guerre psychologique* and to the more vague American concepts of strategic psychological warfare and tactical psychological warfare operations.) The targets for these advertisements are loyal supporters of the regime and that large group of people in the developing states who remain politically apathetic until their lives are directly threatened. These propaganda operations are designed to strengthen morale and induce new allegiance. In short, the objective of these reform activities and the follow-up measures is the psychopolitical mobilization of the populace.

It should be remembered that this objective is also advanced by the insurgents as a primary goal (detachment) in the first phases of their operations and as a secondary goal in the last two phases. Insurgents and incumbents, therefore, will be competing for the same objective. This is as it should be because control of the populace is essential for the success of counterinsurgency, as well as insurgency, warfare.

Nevertheless, the incumbent regime's reforms and its psychological-action operations must not be mere explicit responses to criticisms and accusations made by the insurgents. Reforms that are nothing more than defensive reactions will be viewed by the populace as products of fear and expediency rather than of sincerity. A propaganda campaign designed directly to counter insurgent propaganda constitutes a surrender of initiative by the government to the insurgents. Furthermore, such counterpropaganda has as its target the enemy's propagandists and not the people, the desired target of the first objective. This psychological operation will undoubtedly be viewed by the populace as a sign of insecurity and defeatism. It is therefore absolutely essential that all the government's psychopolitical counterinsurgency operations, in the initiatory period and throughout the war, be oriented in a positive and constructive manner.

In addition to its psychopolitical activities, the government must launch military operations to support the tactic of consolidation and provide a counterattack stance for the armed forces. Normally, the regime's military commander will immediately be faced with a very difficult problem. Since the insurgency is already in its second or third phase and the ratio of troops to guerrillas needed for effective counteraction is known to be about 10:1, he will be confronted at the very outset with a serious lack of resources.

The commander's extreme alternatives for deployment of his limited forces are represented by the opposing concepts of dispersion and concentration. He may disperse his strength throughout the country to protect key villages, installations, and communication hubs. He will undoubtedly be subjected to political pressures calling for dispersals to provide protection to the home regions of important figures in the national government. Or the commander may concentrate his forces in one section of the country in order to gain a sufficient preponderance of strength to defeat decisively the insurgents in that limited area before repeating the operation in the next adjacent sector. This operational concept was employed by General Challe in Algeria after he assumed command of counterinsurgency operations in 1954.[7] To be more than temporarily effective, a sociopolitical victory must be achieved together with the military victory in each sector. Otherwise, as the military commander moves his forces into another target area, the insurgents will reinfiltrate behind him and undo his accomplishments.

The selection of either of these extreme alternatives is generally acceptable to the insurgency leadership. If the former course of action is followed, the guerrillas can selectively bring superior force to bear on numerous defended targets and register a series of military victories. As viewed by the general populace, these victories would tend to portray the insurgent movement as a safer bet for political allegiance than the incumbent regime. If the latter alternative is followed, those sectors from which forces have been withdrawn to permit concentration in a particular area become most vulnerable to complete military occupation by the insurgents. The insurgent organization attempts to place embryonic administrative and executive staff agencies in all areas during Phase One and early Phase Two. It is quite probable, therefore, that full political control could quickly be accomplished in the vacated sectors. With the use of good organizational techniques, it is conceivable that the insurgents could harness the resources of each sector so as to preclude their reoccupation by government forces. The selection of this alternative by the counterinsurgents could inadvertently promote the development of a Communist insurgency from Phase Two to Phase Three or from the third to the final phase of civil war.

Neither of these extreme courses of action is suitable for the achievement of the general objective—increased control of the populace. The appropriate solution, as is the case with so many social problems, lies somewhere between these two extremes. Given the limitations of his available resources, the counterinsurgency commander can best consolidate the regime's holdings by first securing those large population and other strategic centers that are of critical political and military importance to the government and the nation. This operation calls for the breaking up of all Communist and front organizations within these centers and for the incarceration and political rehabilitation of all activists who support the insurgency. This is accomplished by maximum use of police and the deployment of regular army troops in static defense positions around these centers.

Normally, these defended sites, with the possible exception of the national capital, should be manned by fewer troops than would be required for optimum security. This undermanning is designed to provide troops for the creation of regional mobile reserve units and to permit a greater number of important sites to receive some forces for static defense. These mobile units should be given defensive back-up responsibility for specifically assigned strategic sites and should be so deployed as to insure rapid reaction to support requests from these centers.

While providing the most effective consolidation of politico-military strength possible under the circumstances, this establishment of static defense areas and mobile reserve units also places the government's armed forces into a counterattack posture. The mobile reserve units, under certain conditions, could be used for pursuit operations after an attack or for aggressive patrol actions in their general areas of responsibility. They also represent a significant potential for future development into offensive strike forces.

The projection of the government's presence and the providing of security to certain strategically important centers, together with the assumption of a posture providing immediate counterattack and future offensive-strike capabilities, all tend to add a psychopolitical dimension to these military operations. Therefore, these operations and the reform programs of the civil administration combine to provide the government with significant increases in population control during the initiatory phases of its counterinsurgency campaign.

Assumption of the Offensive—The objective of expanding the number of people coming under the control of the incumbent government and diminishing the number of people under insurgent control continues to be a central consideration as the counterinsurgency campaigns assume an offensive character. The incumbent regime must continue to demonstrate its sincerity in meeting the aspirations of the people by instituting additional quick-impact and some long-term programs for sociopolitical reform and economic development.

Segments of the incumbent political élite will undoubtedly resist the implementation of these additional programs. Their motives will be a mixture of a desire to protect and preserve their vested self-interests and an appreciation of the fact that the institution of liberalizing reforms may decrease the government's centralized control over the nation during an emergency situation. They must be made to realize that the previous indulgence of their self-interests has probably contributed to the occurrence of insurgency. In addition, the institution of some political reforms can actually strengthen the government in this time of emergency. Such reforms may lessen incentives for non-Communist dissident élites to go underground and compound the security problems faced by the regime. Furthermore, reforms at local levels can bring more people directly into the political activities relevant to the pursuit of counterinsurgency warfare. Although these reforms may be modest during the emergency period, they must be easily discernible and their results easy to experience. Most important, they must be bona fide harbingers of popularly desired and realistically feasible political liberalization in the postinsurgency period.

The simultaneous conduct of internal war and the implementation of costly long-term development projects will present considerable problems for the central government. The temptation to devote all resources to the immediate task of defeating the insurgency so that substantial constructive programs can be instituted in a peaceful environment will undoubtedly be great within the regime's decision-making circles. It must be resisted, and a balance between the allocation of capital and skills for destructive and constructive purposes must be achieved. Higher priority must be given to the task of defeating the insurgents in military engagement. (However, as will be discussed in Chapter 6, the role of the armed forces need not be exclusively destructive in counterinsurgency operations.) The destructive tasks of defeating the insurgent forces and the constructive task of nation-building must be carried out together as a composite solution to a complex problem.

These developmental operations and reform programs, like those actions instituted earlier during the consolidation and counterattack period, must be fully and continually exploited by psychological means. They must continue to be a part of the standard diet of psychological-action operations directed at all noninsurgents, and these operations must continue to reflect only the truth. Most important, this truth must be substantial enough to generate within the populace a feeling of faith in the government and hope for the future.

Through a proper combination of the solutions to the population control problem prescribed above, results can be increased in exponential fashion. The quantitative and qualitative increases in political support that accrue to the government through the implementation of these prescriptions can be in turn exploited to increase even further the number of people who will pledge their allegiance to the reformist-oriented incumbent regime. The key to this plan is the acquisition of more personnel for the counterinsurgency forces. As noted earlier, a new source of military manpower is gained by the government as additional people commit themselves politically to the regime. These people, both male and female, should be recruited into the regular military and auxiliary components of the government's armed forces. Emphasis should be placed upon incorporating them into militia and paramilitary defense units. After brief training in weapons handling and in the basic tactics of perimeter defense, they can relieve regular army troops who had earlier been assigned static-defense duties at the strategic sites. These professional soldiers in turn can augment the mobile reserve units and thus increase the capability for offensive strike operations. The military imperative of taking the initiative will be achieved for the first time in a meaningful manner by the government's forces.

As this capability grows, the newly created strike forces can extend their activities into the countryside surrounding the secured strategic centers. It will be remembered that the villages in the outlying areas usually contain the bulk of the population. These multiple-pronged, offensive, patrol operations should seek to strengthen the government's control over loyal villages. More important, they must seek to challenge the partial control which the insurgents hold over villages in the twilight zone that exists at some distance from the government's strategic centers. These villages have to be won over completely to the government's cause. A six-element program can be used to achieve this objective. Its components are (1) troop public relations activities, (2) military-civic action programs, (3) informational programs, (4) creation of pacification committees, (5) institution of reward and punishment systems, and (6) provision of physical security to village inhabitants.

Counterinsurgent troops need not view all peasants automatically as guerrillas in disguise. The temptation to do this is naturally great in the frustrating job of constant patrolling under difficult circumstances with minimal contacts with insurgents. If this perverted view is held by the troops, brutality toward civilians will follow in a natural manner and will serve as an inducement to the peasants to join the insurgents for security and retribution.

Even in the absence of such a view, counterinsurgent troops can alienate the general populace in another manner. While on patrol, these troops often believe that they have a general license to expropriate goods and services from village inhabitants without just compensation. A great deficiency of the Philippine government's early counterinsurgency operations was that its troops, while on patrol operations, took over private homes, stole food, forced women to do menial tasks for them, and in general caused great resentment among the civilian populace.[8] Such acts either forced villages into voluntary associations with the insurgents or, if the insurgents themselves were ruthless, forced the inhabitants into a feeling of indifference toward the incumbent-insurgent struggle. In either case the incumbent government became the loser. Such practices cannot be tolerated by higher authority. Counterinsurgent troops should always be prudently cautious, but they should also, by good practices, seek to create within the peasant's mind the image of an honest, friendly, and helpful soldiery.

The second element involves the utilization of the technological, medical, and administrative expertise of the deployed military units in the carrying out of easily discernible and quick-impact community improvement projects.

The third element, a "grass-roots" extension of the government's psychological-action program, calls for the description of government achievements and future plans in sociopolitical reform and economic development. This action can be carried out by the senior military officer present and must be geared to the proper intelligence level of the audience. It should also be personalized so that the villager can appreciate the impact of impending changes upon himself and his progeny. Picture posters and leaflets can be used to remind the inhabitants of the government's programs and their stake in them.

The fourth element calls for the creation of a committee composed of village elders (or elected officials), a civil representative of the central (or provincial) government, and a military representative of the district command. This committee should meet frequently to discuss the village's problems, plan its development, explore the best possible ways of acquiring resources needed to carry out its recommendations, and implement approved programs. The presence of the higher-level civil servant and the military officer will symbolize to the village inhabitants that they are truly an integral part of the national community.

After military and political integration is in fact accomplished and developmental programs are begun, this pacification committee can be converted into a liaison committee which is more advisory than executive or administrative in its functions. Locally elected officials should then assume the administrative and executive burdens within the village.

The institution of a reward and punishment system, the fifth element, is also important to regain government control over villages in the twilight zone. In addition to showing friendliness and concern for the desires of the inhabitants, the government forces must also display firmness and fairness in dealing with these people. The pacification committee, under the direction of the regime's civil or military representative, should provide liberal rewards and personal protection to inhabitants who supply intelligence on insurgent activities. Monetary rewards and decorations can be given to those who excel in their jobs of building fortifications or community improvement projects. The committee must also mete out stringent but legally appropriate punishment to villagers found to be harboring insurgents or supplying them with food or other contraband.

As to punishment, terror must never be used by government forces. The temptation to punish a whole village is great when particularly troublesome insurgents are known to reside within its confines and when the inhabitants are most reluctant to turn them in to government authorities. The inhabitants will generally not act against the insurgents, whom they usually know, because they are afraid of terroristic reprisals by the guerrilla band itself. The solution of counter-terror presents itself logically to the counterinsurgent commander. But the implementation seldom results in anything more than limited and transitory success. It alienates the populace further and adds a long-term retributional dimension to this alienation. More than that, it constitutes the regime's surrender to the insurgents in the fields of policy and ethics.[9] A slower but more lasting and more ethically appropriate solution can be found by providing the villagers with physical security.

The sixth element is specifically designed to provide this security to the villages. At first, it requires the elimination of insurgent infiltrators from the local population. The government's civil servant member of the pacification committee should be responsible for this operation. The other aspect is the protection of the village from external attacks. Initially this calls for the deployment of the mobile reserve forces in such a manner that they can provide defensive cover to the strategic centers and also, in the twilight zone, to those villages that are undergoing this six-element process of political reintegration under the incumbent regime. Most important, this program calls for the construction of fortifications around the village and for the organization and training of paramilitary self-defense forces. These local defense units will then be required to hold off insurgent attacks until the arrival of assistance from the regular military forces. Through these organizational, training, and operational activities, the inhabitants of a village will be brought directly into the incumbent-insurgent conflict, and the government's cause will become more and more their own.

The result of the creation of paramilitary units in certain countryside villages will be further accrual of political power to the government. Still more regular troops can be relieved from static defense billets or even from mobile reserve assignments and can be placed in newly organized offensive strike units. The occasions for more military victories, through increased offensive action, will be increased. The opportunities for bringing more villages out of the twilight zone of dual control and into the incumbent camp will also be increased. And of great significance, the government's military capability for reclaiming those villages beyond this zone and under complete insurgent control will be substantially enhanced.

The progressive application of this six-element procedure for control of village inhabitants will require a long period of time for completion. A short-cut procedure to complement this program, as it is applied to certain villages in the twilight zone, is the technique of resettlement. This will shorten the time the incumbent regime needs to reincorporate the outlying villages, especially those beyond the twilight zone, into the national political fabric. A discussion of resettlement is presented later in this chapter.

The prescriptions provided above, under the subheadings of "Consolidation and Counterattack" and "Assumption of the Offensive," can insure an insurgency-besieged government of a reasonable chance of reaching its all-important objective—expanding its control to cover the entire indigenous populace. Since such control is the ultimate determinant of the outcome of this warfare, this operation alone can theoretically bring victory to the incumbent regime. Again, however, the time required for the completion of this entire program of progressive advances in population control will probably be unacceptable to a government anxious to devote all its resources to meeting the more constructive problems of development to modernity.

The insurgents will not remain passive as this operation is conducted. Their counteractions will further slow it down. To quell completely the insurgency in the shortest possible time, it will be necessary to seek out the enemy forces and destroy them or force them to capitulate in military combat. Besides, what better reinforcement can the incumbent regime provide its psychopolitical program for controlling the populace than military victories over that force which is competing with it for control?

Weakening and Exposure of Guerrilla Forces

In order to expedite the creation of situations which will rationally dictate the engagement of the guerrillas via offensive action, it is necessary indirectly to weaken the guerrilla forces at the same time that the counterinsurgent establishment is being directly strengthened. This can be accomplished in many ways, but the most important technique, ironically enough, stems from the application by the incumbent government of the *yin-yang* concept.

The insurgent military forces' strength is derived to a great extent from an exploitation of its supporters, the uncommitted masses, and the loyal citizens who cannot be protected from the guerrilla bands. Either through choice or through coercion, these people supply the insurgent units with such essentials as intelligence, personnel, food, and clothing. In this strength, however—in the Maoist tradition—there is also an element of weakness. The excessive dependence upon this single collective element of support can be exploited by the counterinsurgents.

Unfortunately for the government, the bulk of these voluntary and nonvoluntary suppliers of resources to the insurgents will reside in the countryside, some distance away from the loci of the regime's strength. The population control operations described above usually will not progress to these more remote areas until the counterinsurgency campaign is well on its way to victory. Faced with this opportunity, but restricted in its actions by limited resources, the government seems to have only one recourse. This is the political-geographical reorganization of the subject regions through resettlement.

In other words, since the government does not have the capability of dispersing and projecting its military strength to cover these important remote settlements and since it cannot afford to wait for its population control operations to reach them, it must bring the inhabitants of these villages to areas which it can directly control. Thus it will weaken the insurgent guerrillas by denying them important sources of logistics and intelligence support. By providing these resettled people with physical protection and by instituting social reforms and economic development projects within their sheltered sites, the government will have an excellent opportunity to gain their complete allegiance.

Resettlement—This technique of weakening guerrillas is not new. Kitchener used it quite effectively against the Boers just prior to the turn of the century. At the insistence of his German military advisers, Chiang Kai-shek employed it against Communist insurgents in the Ching Kang Shan area of south China in 1933. In the 1940's the Japanese attempted to add a new, positive dimension to the negative dimension of denying insurgents access to the villages. This dimension was socioeconomic and political development within the newly established resettlement communities. The Japanese Rural Purification Movement, SEIKYO, was a half-hearted and unsuccessful attempt to apply this new dimension to Japanese counterinsurgent operations in central China.[10]

A special version of the resettlement technique was initiated by Ramón Magsaysay in the Philippines in 1950. His plan, EDCOR (Economic Development Corps), was a major civic endeavor of the Philippine Armed Forces to rehabilitate HUK prisoners. Farm communities were established on Mindanao Island and turned over to these prisoners and their families. Since the HUKS were ostensibly fighting for nothing more than land, this offer of a farm plus a loan to any insurgent who surrendered somewhat undercut the HUK cause. Numerous defections took place from the ranks of the guerrillas and their support personnel. Magsaysay's resettlement plan was thus directed to the separation of land-hungry peasant insurgents from the true Communist insurgents, rather than to the separation of insurgents from the masses as is the normal objective of this technique. This plan was later expanded to include the resettlement of Philippine Army veterans and then nonveteran civilian volunteers.[11]

In 1951, as part of the "Briggs Plan," the British set out to resettle half a million squatters, mostly Chinese, who lived in small communities on the fringes of the jungle in Malaya.[12] These people included both willing and unwilling supporters of the Communist insurgents. The use of this technique in Malaya was a most important factor in the dampening out of the insurgency. It was also extremely effective when employed by the French against the Vietminh in Cambodia during 1951–1952, but not so effective when later used by them against the FLN in Algeria. A rather poorly managed version, under the code designation of "Operation Sunrise," was used extensively and apparently with mixed success in South Vietnam during the latter stages of the Diem regime.

Resettlement must be used in a cautious manner because the removal of peasants from their traditional home sites and the destruction of their dwellings (so the guerrillas cannot use them) automatically cause these people to experience serious social and physical stresses. It tends to compromise at the very outset, at least as viewed by an affected peasant, the government's announced goals for such a program. These goals are increased opportunities for socioeconomic development and physical protection of the individual and his property. It is imperative, therefore, for the government to do everything necessary to make the operation as humane as is possible.

The officials responsible for a particular resettlement project must try to convince the affected peoples, through speeches and patient discussion, of the benefits to them and their children as a result of their relocation. In many cases, however, it will be wise literally to capture the audience for this briefing and then immediately follow up with the implementation of the program. The reason is that if advance notice is given, many inhabitants in these villages will be gone when the government officials arrive.[13] They will hide in the forest until the operation is completed and then will return to rebuild a home on their ancestral land.

After the briefing, the inhabitants can be permitted to place all of their removable property on vehicles provided by the government for transport to their new home site. An evaluation is then made of the worth of each dwelling, of each family's crops, and of other personal property to be destroyed. On-the-spot compensation is provided to the dispossessed owners in currency if this is at all possible. The entire process of destroying the old villages and of moving the inhabitants must be carefully supervised to preclude chaotic riot-breeding situations. It is important that the government's project team include medical personnel and social workers to assist the people in solving personal problems raised by the resettlement process.

The site of the new settlement should, of course, be selected well in advance of the actual movement of people. The principal determinant in site selection is a location that can easily be defended. Preferably it should be on government-owned lands that show high promise for productive cultivation. Other considerations are the proximity of the site to communications lines and to additional sources of employment (mines, plantations), and the potential of the site for satisfy-

ing the increased requirements for productive land, requirements that will come with future growth and development.

The government can give or sell (at a very generous price)
a home site and a plot of workable land to each family that
has been moved to the resettlement area. It must then provide
the technicians, equipment, and certain manufactured materials necessary for the community self-help projects of
building private homes, schools, civic buildings, clinics, and
marketplaces. It should staff the clinics and schools and provide the technicians needed to maintain other social services
and to aid the farmers in the planting of their new crops.
Having done all of this, in order to complete each such project
the government need only implement those internal organization and security aspects of the six-element village population control plan.

The creation of such resettlement villages will effectively
deny the insurgents contacts with previously accessible and
exploitable people. The guerrilla units will be weakened by
the consequent diminution of personnel, logistic, and informational support from these sources.[14] Of almost equal importance, a government-sponsored social revolution can occur
within these villages with the result that many of the causes
of insurgency, factors of socioeconomic instability, will concurrently be eliminated.

Cut-off of External Aid—It was noted in the preceding
chapter that Phase Two and Three of Communist insurgency
may be marked by the supply of external aid from friendly
Communist states. Employing only its own resources, the incumbent regime will find this a most difficult problem to solve.
The counterinsurgent forces have, in theory, four solutions
available to them in employing their ground forces if aid is
brought in via overland routes from a contiguous Communist
state into an insurgent base area: (1) a long-range assault
penetration of the insurgent base area to be followed by its
occupation; (2) continual, long-range patrol activities by large

heavily armed units along the affected border; (3) the deployment to the border area of small, self-sustaining, military special forces teams to conduct guerrilla-type warfare along the supply trails; and (4) the systematic and progressive consolidation of the rear and all other regions bordering on the base area prior to a general assault on the guerrilla redoubt.

The first two solutions require a well-developed logistics system capable of sustained, long-range operations. A developing state usually does not have such a system. If it is forced to rely on indigenous capabilities alone, these solutions must be rejected. The third and fourth solutions, on the other hand, appear feasible and can be employed simultaneously.

The special forces units, which can live off the land and require only minimal support from the rear-area establishment, do not possess a capability in themselves for destroying this enemy logistics system. Nevertheless, through frequent ambushes of guerrilla supply columns, they could significantly disrupt the operations of the system.

If the target state has a seacoast and if the insurgents receive their externally supplied aid by sea, then three courses of action must be followed: (1) naval vessels, augmented by fishing boats manned by trained naval militia, must conduct continual sea patrols to initiate periodic searches of indigenous fishing vessels and to intercept all foreign vessels headed for unauthorized ports; (2) a comprehensive port inspection system for all incoming cargo must be implemented to preclude illegal entry of contraband goods; and (3) if adequate manpower is available, militia units should patrol those coastal strips which could for many reasons be logical discharge points for contraband.[15]

Another action for the incumbent regime, regardless of the mode of external supply to the insurgents, is the harnessing of all possible diplomatic pressure and bringing it to bear on the involved Communist state in an attempt to force it to terminate its illicit activities.

Psychological Warfare Operations—The guerrilla, despite

his heavy and continuing diet of political-ideological training, is still quite susceptible to his opponent's psychological warfare operations. He is often on the retreat; he must continually avoid pitched battles with a stronger enemy; he lives under great physical and psychological strain; finally, he seldom has the opportunity, especially during Phase Two, to evaluate realistically the success of his efforts. Thus he tends, despite the exhortations of his political commissar, to believe wild rumors and to experience rapid changes in his morale.

One aspect of the counterinsurgent forces' psychological warfare operations can be directed at undercutting the insurgents' reasons for fighting. Magsaysay's EDCOR program was designed for this very purpose. Another aspect can point out that the insurgency faces inevitable defeat, that the guerrillas are living their miserable, hunted lives in vain, and that unless they surrender nothing awaits them but death.

These two aspects should be followed up by a positive inducement campaign. Offers of amnesty and rehabilitation can be extended to the rank and file and timed to coincide with general public appeals by families and friends to "come home."

In all these operations much information can be obtained from the captured insurgents. Where possible, propaganda should be directed at individual bands or groups of insurgents where the use of names is most effective. Captured insurgents who have been rehabilitated can also make direct personal appeals to their former comrades through leaflets or radio broadcasts.

Still another aspect of psychological warfare operations involves specialized disruption campaigns. It will be remembered that Phase Two Communist insurgency is characterized by a lack of centralized control over many closely knit, small guerrilla bands. This encourages local-leader initiative and the development of personal loyalties to the immediate leader. This in turn tends to create a spirit of competition among these bands while, within the bands, it creates general distrust for all outsiders. These conditions indicate that Phase Two insurgency is pregnant with manifold opportunities for disruptive exploitation by the counterinsurgents' psychological warfare operations.

Phase Three may very well include destabilizing demotions of senior officers and promotions of junior officers as the movement attempts to find leaders qualified for the more complex and intellectually demanding staff and command positions at district and regional levels. Every attempt must be made to acquire all possible data on such personnel problems so that this information can be utilized to sow distrust and discontent within the insurgent organization. Special emphasis can be placed on those units which had sent one of their fine combat officers up to higher headquarters only to have him returned a short time later as a man unfit for higher responsibilities.

The announcement of high rewards for various guerrilla leaders is a useful disruptive measure. These leaders often grow suspicious of new guerrilla recruits in their command; they become more distrustful of adjacent units; and, as a result, they begin restricting their movements and decreasing their unit's aggressiveness.

The choice of vehicles for transmitting psychological warfare messages to the insurgents is, of course, determined by existing communications media. The anti-Communist insurgent campaigns in Malaya and in the Philippines indicate that if the proper instrument is chosen for a given situation the results—as measured in terms of a drop in enemy morale, a diminution of guerrilla unit aggressiveness, and an increase in surrenders—can significantly weaken the insurgent forces.

Intelligence—The techniques of resettlement, cut-off of external aid, and psychological warfare operations are all designed directly to weaken the enemy by denying him the necessary physical, material, and psychological resources needed to carry on guerrilla warfare. Some of these techniques force the guerrilla troops into exposing themselves on more occasions and on a greater scale if they are to survive as military units.

They are compelled more and more to launch attacks of a substantial size to insure a successful breach of the newly fortified, traditional, domestic sources of supply. As the requirements for such supplies continue to grow in anticipation of further development of the insurgency, the frequency of these large-scale attacks must be increased. In short, proper use of the above-mentioned techniques can force an insurgency to move prematurely into advanced phase operations as a result of the need to survive rather than as a result of careful planning and preparation. This constitutes general exposure. Through good intelligence, precise locational exposure can be obtained so that the government's forces can engage insurgent units in decisive battles.

It goes almost without saying that a friendly populace, a well-organized paramilitary system, an effective regular military establishment, and an imaginative internal security system will probably discourage the initiation of insurgencies in the first place. These standard general sources of intelligence usually will not be fully developed in an emerging state when it is first confronted with Communist insurgency. Even if they are fully developed, additional tactical information is needed for effective planning and operations.

Certain specialized sources and actions can be employed to obtain a nearly complete picture of the insurgency in its overt combat phases. Full exploitation of surrendered insurgent personnel is an extremely important aspect of the government's intelligence-collection activities. An interesting statistical sidelight is that in the last four years of the Malayan Emergency the intelligence gathered from each surrender usually resulted in the death of two insurgents.

Needed intelligence can also be acquired by infiltration of the insurgent base itself. This is a risky endeavor, but it may pay handsome dividends if properly carried out. By carefully creating evidence to corroborate a given cover-up story for an infiltrator, the Philippine Army's Military Intelligence Service was able to place an agent directly inside the inner circle of the HUK headquarters on Mt. Arayat. This agent was made the bodyguard of Taruc, the leader of the HUK field forces. He supplied the government with the first current photographs of HUK leaders and furnished information that led to the apprehending of 1,175 members of the HUK's logistic support organization, the National Finance Committee. He was thus personally responsible for the destruction of the complex and essential supply line of the HUK guerrilla forces.

Another form of infiltration, and usually a consistent producer of intelligence, is the deep penetration reconnaissance patrol. Such patrols may be carried out by intelligence-collection units with only a self-defense combat capability, or they may be performed by units which have a dual capability that permits them to exploit directly, by offensive action, the intelligence they have collected. The Filipino Scout Ranger team is an excellent example of the former, and the British "special platoon" of the Malaya Emergency period is an example of the latter. Sometimes the dual-capability forces disguise themselves to appear like the insurgent bands they are seeking.

The old form of fixed-station observation and the newer varieties of motor, electronic, and infrared reconnaissance should also be used whenever the capability is present and the situation is favorable. It is axiomatic that all reconnaissance units possess a communications capability to permit them quickly to forward reports to intelligence-collection centers without leaving their operational area.

The intelligence-collection and evaluation centers can play a most important role in counterinsurgency warfare. The creation of such centers was first called for in the German Army's *Manual on Warfare Against Bands for all Services of the Armed Forces* (1944).[16] This work, it should be noted, was based on the Germans' extensive experience in fighting partisan-guerrillas during the Second World War. Later, the British counterinsurgency forces in Malaya, Cyprus, and Kenya found the establishment of such intelligence activities a great asset to their operations. Hence the creation of this sort of center strongly suggests itself to any state engaged in military operations against guerrilla units.

For greatest utility and efficiency, these centers can be organized on a pyramidal basis under a single civilian or military commander. Necessary civil-military coordination will be enhanced considerably if the military operational sectors are physically situated at the seats of district and provincial civil administration. Each civil and military agency with an intelligence-collection mission, ranging from a village policeman to an army reconnaissance unit, must report to such a center. Dissemination of raw data with immediate exploitation authority should be granted to the operational commander working with the intelligence center receiving a report of a target of opportunity. Thus the chances for engaging the enemy, no matter how brief his exposure, will be considerably enhanced. Each engagement forced upon the guerrilla forces in Phase Two or Three which is not the result of their calculations stands an excellent chance of resulting in a victory for the counterinsurgent forces and a further diminution of insurgent strength.

Foreign Assistance—The incumbent government generally is in a much better position to secure external assistance than is the insurgent organization. Through its embassies, it has direct contact with those states desiring to supply it with assistance. If it has international alliances, its chances of receiving such aid may be greatly enhanced. By virtue of its control over major transportation and communications hubs, it can facilitate the delivery of material aid to its supply centers. It appears to follow logically that the incumbent regime should fully exploit this advantage to add to its strength and thus indirectly, and in a relative manner, weaken the insurgent forces.

In utilizing this advantage, however, there is a danger that must be appreciated before such aid is solicited. By accepting extensive economic and military support and especially by permitting the supplier state's technicians and advisers to enter the country in great numbers, the government will automatically invite the insurgent propagandists to label it a foreign puppet regime. Even if the insurgents are receiving outside assistance, the means are generally covert and the supply and training centers distant from the population centers. The government's counteraccusation will have little impact upon the populace. In some states the psychological liability that the incumbent government will incur when it accepts substantial amounts of military-economic aid may outweigh its material benefits.

In those cases where such aid is determined to be feasible and essential and where external support is furnished, the government's new strength must be carefully employed if it is to contribute to a lasting solution to the insurgency problem. It must be applied to alleviate the socioeconomic grievances of the general populace and to defeat the guerrilla forces in military combat.

Engagement and Defeat of the Guerrilla Forces

The most fundamental principle to be applied to counterinsurgency warfare during Phases Two and Three of Communist insurgency is the gaining and retention of initiative. The tactics of offense are an imperative if victory is to be attained. The partial achievement of the goals of expanding control over greater portions of the populace and the weakening and exposing of the enemy will give the incumbent forces the capability and the opportunity to take the offensive. Thus the government will be in a position to take action leading to the achievement of the third goal, the defeat of the enemy's field forces, the guerrilla units.

With greater numbers of troops to be employed for offensive strikes, with an increasing capability for the mobility of his forces, and with the improvement of intelligence on the enemy, the counterinsurgent commander must decide how to employ his strength most effectively against the insurgent's operational field units. His basic tactical alternatives are large- and small-scale operations.

Large-Scale Operations—Much of the literature on guerrilla warfare, at the time of this writing, contains numerous endorsements of encirclement as a most effective tactic in counterguerrilla warfare. Most likely these endorsements stem primarily from the successes registered by the Germans in using this maneuver against partisan forces in Europe during World War II.

German successes normally can be attributed either to the extensive size or to the inhabited and developed nature of the encircled region. In order to encircle a large area effectively, it is necessary to have many well-trained troops and an excellent mobility capability to permit the rapid and instantaneous deployment of these forces from their normal bases to the "stop" or assembly points of the encircling line. The predominance of inhabited and culturally developed characteristics greatly aids this process: the more easily defined reference points can be established and the, relatively speaking, untangled and easily circumscribed nature of the terrain facilitates systematic and precise search operations.

An analysis of these factors against a backdrop of typical conditions within the underdeveloped states of Asia, Africa, and Latin America suggests that encirclement will not meet with equal success when applied in these areas. First, the military establishment in a developing state will not normally contain a sufficient number of well-trained troops to carry out effectively this maneuver and to perform concurrently other essential duties in Phase Two or Three insurgency situations. Second, this establishment will not normally possess an adequate mobility capability necessary for such operations if they are to be efficiently executed. (However, it may acquire such a capability from an ally—as the Republic of Vietnam did in the Vietcong insurgency.) Third, the very nature of the terrain occupied by guerrillas in these states precludes effective combing of the area as the circle is contracted. Fourth, the guerrillas, especially in their specific base areas, enjoy the capability of being able to transform themselves quickly into peaceful peasants; and the advance warning afforded the insurgents through the elaborate and massive preparations required to implement this maneuver tends to insure that all guerrillas will see the need for this action.

Even if adequate, well-trained forces and a mobility capability do exist, the counterinsurgent forces may very well be unsuccessful because of the third factor alone. This was the consistent experience of the British forces in their war against the Communist MRLA in Malaya. If the forces and mobility capability are present, this tactic may also prove ineffective when faced with the fourth factor alone. Such was the equally consistent experience of the French Army in its war against the Vietminh. It follows naturally that the presence of all four factors virtually denies this tactic any reasonable utility in underdeveloped states. The Burmese Army's experiences in its conflict with Communist insurgent bands in the early 1950's testify to this.[17]

The sweep is perhaps even less effective than the large-scale encirclement and search maneuver. It consists of launching one or more waves of troops in a direct combing exercise that will cover a prescribed area in the shortest possible time consistent with thorough search. Because of generally good local intelligence in their base areas and again because of the massive preparations required prior to the execution of this tactic, guerrillas are usually able to avoid the sweepers by either drawing out of their path or advancing beyond the terminal point. After the sweep is completed, the government forces return to their stations exhausted with little in the way of successful engagements to compensate for these expenditures of energy and matériel. The guerrillas also return to their swept area confident that they will be free from molestation for some time to come. French, British, and Filipino counterinsurgency forces discovered the futility of this maneuver in the 1950's; the South Vietnamese Army, somewhat hampered by the legacy of its French training, experienced this same futility in the early 1960's.

Large-scale tactics not only will fail to produce military victories but also will result in psycho-political defeats. When the government deploys a large force of troops against a handful of guerrillas and fails, the insurgents automatically gain considerable stature in the eyes of the populace, who then also may begin to doubt the power of the incumbent regime to win.

Small-Scale Operations—These operations, unlike those described above, can be readily tailored to the peculiarities of insurgency war in the developing areas. They normally call for capabilities that are inherent in an indigenous military establishment; they permit the counterinsurgent forces maximum flexibility, surprise, and continued initiative; even if they fail on occasion, their failure is less noticeable and less discouraging to loyal members of the public.

Small-scale operations can be carried out principally by hunter-killer units of uniformed Ranger-trained regular troops operating out of fixed fortified bases dispersed throughout guerrilla-affected areas. These fixed installations are not to be used in static-defense roles to protect certain locations; rather, they are to serve as support installations for the constantly active patrol operations of the combat units. Their sole purpose is to promote the mobility of the counterinsurgency forces.

Once assigned to a particular fixed base and hence to an associated and specifically delineated patrol-zone, each hunter-killer unit can begin its exploitation operations against guerrillas in its assigned area. Such operations may involve a direct attack on an encampment of insurgent forces or a semi-permanent supply center, or it may call for the ambush of an insurgent column. The central aims of this action are to surprise the insurgents; force them to engage the unit under the latter's own terms; annihilate by highly disciplined and massed fire as many guerrillas as possible; and confiscate or

destroy all captured matériel. This last point should not be
overlooked, for, depending on the phase of development of
the insurgency, the confiscation or destruction of these weapons may be more significant than the destruction of insurgent
personnel.

Pseudo-bands, the counterinsurgent forces' nonuniformed
guerrilla units, can also be organized and trained to carry out
the same small-scale operations as the hunter-killer teams;
but their operational sectors will include only those areas
where insurgent control is exceptionally strong. Through their
disguises these units appear to be insurgent bands. Thus they
are able to obtain vital information from villagers who normally cooperate with the guerrilla forces.

During Phase Two insurgency, when communication and
coordination among guerrilla bands are virtually nonexistent,
these pseudo-bands can join with the insurgents and collect
such invaluable information as tactical doctrine and organization, to name a few, and, of course, at the appropriate time
they can destroy the insurgent unit. The brilliant exploits of
the Filipino Army's "Force X" against HUK guerrillas in the
Candaba Swamp is an excellent example of this operation.
The equally brilliant achievements of the British Army's Major
Kitson and his "pseudo-gangs" of reformed Mau Mau terrorists
in Kenya is another case in point.

A final analysis of the tactics available to counterinsurgent
commanders who have the capability of assuming the offense
indicates that small-scale operations have a more direct application to solving the problems of engaging and defeating
guerrilla forces than do large-scale actions. These operations
can generally be carried out with resources available to the
indigenous military establishment. By providing the counterinsurgent forces with a high degree of mobility and a continual capability for surprise attack, they can also surmount
the impediments to effective search posed by difficult terrain
and by the chameleon-like quality of the peasant guerrilla.
They permit the counterinsurgent forces to gain and retain

the initiative, to restrict the maneuvering area of the insurgent units, and to compel these units to fight under the terms prescribed by their opponents. In a broader context, even when contact and engagement do not occur, these operations force the guerrillas to be off balance, to be on the move constantly, and to be generally incapable of regaining any offensive momentum.

In many cases of future insurgency, the surface operations discussed above may well be the only action that an incumbent government may be able or perhaps willing to take to defeat Communist guerrilla forces. In other cases the capability of the government for achieving the three principal objectives of counterguerrilla warfare may be enhanced by the addition of a more advanced form of sea power to the regime's military establishment. More important, it is our contention that, given the general characteristics of this type of combat, surface operations may be supplemented in a decisive fashion through the employment of airpower.

6

Air Operations
and General Organization

The proper utilization of airpower by a government beset with insurgency can significantly aid the incumbent forces in the attainment of the three principal objectives of counter-guerrilla warfare. Airpower properly coordinated with surface power plus highly coordinated military and civil agency operations can insure the defeat of the insurgent guerrillas in military combat.

Control of the Populace

According to an earlier prescription, the first actions to be taken by a government—once it decides to respond in a concerted manner to intermediate phase Communist insurgency —are the consolidation of its holdings over national strategic centers and the assumption of a counterattack posture. Through the use of aircraft, troop and equipment deployments to these centers can be quickly accomplished. The assignment of air carriers to the mobile reserve forces, which are also formed at this time, will greatly decrease the reaction time needed to get these units to the reconsolidated areas coming under insurgent attack. These aircraft will significantly increase the effective range of the forces, thus permitting many population centers to come under their defensive, protective cover.

Once the offensive is assumed in the population control programs and elements of these mobile reserve forces are sent out to the peripheral villages in the twilight zone, the air vehicles can aid in solving transportation problems. They can again provide quick reaction times for emergency requests from newly fortified villages. These requests might range from supplies of foodstuffs or medical goods or a replacement part for the village water pump to military support such as airborne troopers, rocket fire, or night-illumination flares to aid the paramilitary units in their defense against attacking insurgent forces.

Airpower can also be used in psychological action programs. As a result of American success in airborne-transmitted educational television, it has been suggested that the incumbent government employ a specially equipped transport aircraft for psychological action programs directed at government-secured villages. The airborne-transmitted programs could cover such topics as solutions to typical indigenous agricultural and water problems, road construction, first aid, and reading; intermingled with this could be official explanations of government reform and development programs and national news items. One or two receivers in each fortified or resettlement village might pay handsome dividends to the incumbent regime in its attempts to raise living standards and concurrently combat the insurgent's overt and covert activities in the rural areas.

It is apparent then that airpower can make a modest but meaningful contribution toward the attainment of the strategic objective of population control.

Weakening and Exposure of the Guerrilla Forces

Foreign Assistance—Brigadier General Jamie Gough, USAF, has suggested certain criteria to be used to determine the acceptability and feasibility of particular aircraft for counterinsurgency warfare. These criteria are functions of the fundamental characteristics of this type of conflict: the extreme importance of the populace, the underdeveloped nature of the battleground areas, the absence of significant enemy airpower, the lack of sophisticated insurgent weapons, the fleeting nature of targets, and the very limited numbers of highly qualified, technically trained personnel within the counterinsurgents' air establishment.

In applying these characteristics to determine the optimum performance criteria for an aircraft to be used in counterinsurgency strike missions, General Gough arrived at some logical and significant conclusions. For example, the strategic objective of protecting the people is of paramount importance in counterinsurgency operations; therefore, the air weapon-system selected should have pinpoint accuracy in the delivery of highly selective munitions. A strike can be considered effective only if the delivered munitions impact upon the enemy alone.

As the battlegrounds for counterguerrilla operations will be centered in the developing areas, it can be safely assumed that the affected regions will probably lack sufficient modern airfields to support sustained air operations. Hence the air weapon-system selected should be of the STOL (short take-off and landing) type.

Because of the absence of significant enemy airpower, the selected aircraft need have only a minimum capability for dealing with the enemy's counter-air threat. This will permit the aircraft to be optimized for its main tasks of close support, reconnaissance, and interdiction.

The fleeting nature of the targets demands that the air

weapon-system have the capability to fly low and slow so that the targets can be more easily found and kept constantly in sight. Two-place aircraft, permitting an airborne observer to fly on each mission, will obviously facilitate visual target acquisition. Having to fly low and slow, however, suggests two-engine-type aircraft with armor plating to minimize danger from ground fire.

Finally, according to General Gough, the aircraft selected should be easy to maintain so that the limited technical expertise of the local national air force will be sufficient to permit sustained operations of these aircraft without excessive assistance from foreign technicians.[1]

The counterinsurgent air force commander will do well to keep these criteria in mind when requesting specific air weapon-systems from a modern power. He should also remember that post-World War II history of counterinsurgency warfare suggests that airpower will be in greater demand in its support roles in reconnaissance and assault airlift missions than in its role of delivering munitions on specific enemy targets.

Resettlement—In its direct application, airpower can aid resettlement in the same way that it assists the fortified villages—quick-reaction deliveries of either constructive or destructive support items.

Indirectly, however, in combination with fortified and resettlement villages, airpower makes a substantial contribution by forcing the enemy units to expose themselves. The very knowledge of an incumbent airborne mobile reserve force compels the enemy to assemble more personnel to assure a rapid and complete breach of the village's static-defense system and a thorough, forceful exploitation of its inhabitants in the shortest possible time. At the same time his knowledge of the government forces' aerial reconnaissance capability compels him to do just the opposite. Hence he is confronted with a disconcerting dilemma that may very well breed overcaution into his planning and assault actions, and overcaution normally leads to frustrations that take the edge off tactical operations of this sort.

Persistent frustrations may well compel guerrilla units to move further back into more remote regions in hopes of exploiting those villages still outside the government's direct control. As the resettlement plan expands its scope, however, opportunities for extracting support from the inhabitants of these hinterland villages will continue to diminish.

Cut-off of External Aid—In our earlier discussion we noted that a long-range assault penetration of a guerrilla base area contiguous to a Communist state would be virtually impossible without a complementary long-range logistics system. Airpower must provide this system with close air support and quickly and efficiently transport the assault force to its target area.

If a lack of resources—ground or air—precludes such an operation, air transports can be used for the delivery of Ranger-trained regular army units or small, self-sustaining special forces teams to border areas between the Communist state and the insurgency-affected nation. These units can be used on patrol operations leading to a general harassment of the enemy's international supply network and can be periodically supplied by airdrop. During the early phases of a counter-insurgency campaign, the government may feel that it cannot afford to spare troops for such border operations. Even if they are available, the number required for effective patrol may prove prohibitive in terms of continual support. Armed aerial reconnaissance, on the other hand, can be a very feasible way of carrying out such a program without an excessive expenditure of manpower and other support resources. Certain specific areas that either lend themselves to ease of transit from one side of the border to the other or are natural junctions of existing road and trail systems or have a history of use for illicit operations should be given special attention on these armed reconnaissance missions.

As this aerial patrol activity begins to take its toll of daylight supply-column movements, the insurgents undoubtedly will resort exclusively to night operations and to keeping repair crews constantly on alert near the bridges and passes needed for transit. Thus a night capability for these armed reconnaissance aircraft is dictated so that repair crews can be harassed in their work and general movement across the border can be detected and interdicted. Flare drops over suspected transit sites can provide a partial but not wholly satisfactory solution to this problem of target acquisition at night. A more satisfactory solution can probably be found in improved "moving target indicator" equipment which can detect even small groups of human beings and pack animals. It is precisely in situations such as this that modern technology should be used to the fullest to solve the traditional problem of night vision.

In lieu of the development and acquisition of a good night visual detection system, the use of high-speed aircraft on armed reconnaissance missions at dusk and daybreak along known logistic lines can prove quite effective. Unwarned by the approach sound of jet aircraft, supply columns are easy targets just as they are going into or emerging from cover. The French used this technique with reasonable success against FLN supply lines from Tunisia to Algeria.[2] Developing nations in possession of a few Korean-war-vintage jet aircraft will do well to follow this technique in comparable situations.

Of course, aerial patrol missions can be flown in support of programs designed to preclude illicit entry of supplies via the water and air approaches to a state. Given the air and sea transport capabilities of the Soviet Union and to a lesser degree Communist China, plus the fact that an overwhelming number of developing states do not possess borders contiguous with these Communist powers, it seems obvious that air and sea will be the media for the covert delivery of assistance to insurgent bands in future Communist-sponsored internal wars.

It is interesting that the Soviets have a significant backlog of experience in carrying out air support missions for guerrilla bands. They had an elaborate organization and conducted extensive operations in supplying material and, most important, leadership cadres to their partisan forces behind German lines during the Second World War. According to German General Karl D. Drum (General der Flieger), the Soviets employed the following units: (1) transport aircraft regiments of the civilian air fleet; (2) units of the long-range bomber organizations; (3) nightfighter regiments; (4) special courier and liaison aircraft groups assigned to individual sectors of the front and used for supplying partisans in addition to flying courier missions; (5) special groups employed in various sectors when necessary, their mission being exclusively to supply partisans, with strength generally corresponding to that of a squadron; and (6) glider regiments.[3]

The Soviets were similarly successful in air support missions to the Pathet Lao forces in the 1960–1962 period. In the absence of a counter-air capability in the possession of the Royal Laotian government, Soviet transport aircraft were able to deliver substantial material aid and North Vietnamese technicians to the Communist insurgent (Pathet Lao) forces.

The lessons of history and the necessities of geography appear to dictate that airpower will have considerable utility in cutting off external aid to those insurgency-besieged states which do not share boundaries with Communist states.

Psychological Warfare—The application of airpower to counterinsurgency operations in itself constitutes a psychological warfare operation. Constant aerial reconnaissance patrols by themselves can have an unnerving effect upon guerrillas; this is especially true when these air patrols supplement the ground operations of hunter-killer units. The expenditure of munitions against insurgent concentrations, whether the direct killing effect is significant or not, also obviously has a psychological impact upon guerrillas who find themselves defenseless against such air attacks. For example, while "Field Marshal" Kimathis claimed that British bombing raids on

Mau Mau targets netted only nine insurgent deaths in twelve months of operations, he neglected to note that the rebel surrender rate increased tremendously during this same period.[4] Such a reaction is not restricted to native peoples, for an exhaustive study of partisan warfare in the Soviet Union during World War II indicates that German antipartisan air attacks, as few as they were in number, caused guerrilla morale to be strained to the utmost, frequently resulting in panic, even during a nonattack reconnaissance fly-over.[5] Additional corroborative evidence of this type of guerrilla reaction to air strikes and fly-overs can be found in an analysis of British operations against the MRLA insurgents.

A more direct way of employing airpower in psychological warfare techniques is the distribution of leaflets by airdrop throughout all areas under insurgent control. Another direct technique, first introduced in 1953 by the British forces in Malaya, is the "voice flight."[6] In such operations aircraft are equipped with loudspeaker transmitting equipment and are flown directly over known insurgent camps. These aircraft orbit a target site and, by means of tape or live broadcasts, flood the area with audible psychological warfare messages. Insurgent leaders can partially counter the impact of leaflet drops in areas by threatening punishment to anyone found reading them, but there is no apparent guerrilla defense against "voice flight" activities. Successful British experiences with this operation in Kenya and Malaya suggest its incorporation into the counterinsurgency forces' psychological warfare programs.[7]

Intelligence—The role of airpower in this particular program, which is designed to weaken the enemy and precisely expose him so that he may be effectively engaged, is essentially that of performing aerial reconnaissance. These operations may vary in nature, depending upon the types of aircraft and related equipment available to the counterinsurgents. They can range from high-speed and high-altitude reconnaissance strikes flown by modern jet aircraft equipped with high resolution, standard and infrared photographic devices to low-slow visual reconnaissance missions by antiquated biplanes.

In the early states of an incumbent regime's response to intermediate phase Communist insurgency, before its population control programs have started bearing fruitful results, intelligence acquired by aerial reconnaissance may well be the only source of this vital commodity available to the government forces. As has been demonstrated in the past histories of numerous post-World War II internal wars, it will remain an important source throughout the counterinsurgency campaign. The acquisition and employment of airpower for this role alone strongly recommends itself to an insurgency-affected developing state.

Engagement and Defeat of the Guerrilla Forces

Attack (strike), airborne assault, and transport operations dominate the contributions of airpower to the achievement of this goal. It goes without saying, however, that the aerial reconnaissance missions flown in pursuit of weakening and exposing the guerrillas play an important part in providing the necessary intelligence to insure that these three operations are most effective in engaging and defeating the enemy.

Air Attack (Strike) Operations—The diminutive and fleeting characteristics of most potential interdiction targets tend to restrict the role of airpower in this aspect of strike operations. A review of typical South Vietnamese Air Force (VNAF) communiqués on its operations against the Vietcong graphically portrays the scope and nature of such actions:

July 12, 1962—Two Viet Nam Air Force AD-6 planes strafed a Viet Cong meeting place seven kilometres northwest of Cai Nuoc, in Xuyen province, for 15 minutes Tuesday afternoon, killing five Viet Cong, a VP correspondent reported.
The day before three AD-6's bombed another Viet Cong area

22 kms. north northwest of Ta Lai, Long Khanh province. Ten houses where Viet Cong were hiding were destroyed.

July 20, 1962—Two AD-6's, two T-28's, and a B-26 raided a Viet Cong troop concentration 20 kms. southwest of Moc Hoa, provincial capital of Kien Tuong. First reports said the Viet Cong left behind 25 killed.

—The same day, a B-26 and a T-28 raided another Viet Cong base 72 kms. southwest of Quang Nagi. Twenty-nine structures were destroyed.[8]

The occasions for employing attack aircraft in close air support activities are somewhat restricted by the small, fleeting nature of targets and by the terrain features that normally will predominate in guerrilla-infested areas. Most important, guerrillas tend to mingle with or cling to civilians when they come under air attack. Thus the problems of safe and politically meaningful ground support impose additional restrictions on such operations.

As the fortified-villages program and resettlement progress, the guerrillas will find it more difficult to use this cling technique because of their consequent isolation from the peasants. Engagements between hunter-killer units and guerrilla patrols will frequently occur in regions located between those government-controlled communities. Close air support will gain in importance as the control of population projects progress.

To enforce the validity and appropriateness of certain prescriptions, many of the above-mentioned historical illustrations deal with the employment of conventional aircraft. One reason is simply that higher-performance air vehicles were not generally available to the counterinsurgents when these particular engagements occurred. It must also be admitted that within the international air force community at large during the very late 1940's and early and mid-1950's a prejudice existed against the use of high-performance aircraft in counterinsurgency operations.

The air officer commanding in Malaya, responding to the

necessity that he possess a general war capability as well as a counterinsurgency capability, rose above the prejudice in 1954. Jet-propelled Vampires, Venoms, and Canberras replaced the piston-driven Hornets and Lincolns in his RAF units. A professional evaluation of the effectiveness of these jet-propelled aircraft in counterinsurgency attack operations is accurately summed up in this statement by an RAF senior officer:

> . . . trials using jet aircraft in the strike role proved entirely successful, and from 1954 onwards jets have been employed on hundreds of strike operations in Malaya with the result that the feasibility of employing the present generation of high-performance fighter and bomber aircraft in this role has been demonstrated beyond doubt.[9]

This testimony to the efficacy of high-performance aircraft in counterguerrilla attack roles appears, upon first thought, to contradict the earlier stated requirement that low-slow capable aircraft should be used for such operations. This, however, is not the case. The jet-propelled aircraft employed by the British had a reasonably good capability for low and slow operations for limited periods of time despite the fact that they were designed for high-performance actions. Ideally speaking, low-performance aircraft are best suited for counterguerrilla strikes because they can spend more time per sortie in a low-slow flight configuration over the target area than can their jet counterparts. Nevertheless, British experience in Malaya —and French experience in Algeria, for that matter—indicates that high-performance air vehicles can indeed be successfully employed in attacks against guerrilla bands.

Transport Operations—As noted earlier, such operations play a key role in the implementation of population control programs. Air carrier missions also can play an indirect but important role in the attainment of the goal to meet and defeat the enemy.

Transport air vehicles, both fixed-wing and rotary-wing types, can be used to provide steady supplies of matériel and personnel to the advanced, static, fortified posts that serve as bases for hunter-killer patrol units. Units that must traverse much difficult terrain even before reaching their assigned patrol zones can be transported by helicopters from their base to that area, thus permitting virtually all time in the field to be devoted to productive patrolling.

Helicopters can also be used for the evacuation of sick or wounded members of the patrol units in the field. This service can result in the saving of lives, the creating of high morale within the deployed forces, and the continuance of a patrol's activities when otherwise it would have been forced to return to base prematurely with its casualties.

Transports can be employed in airdrop resupply operations to provide logistics service to these units. In special cases they may be used to bring in special weapons too heavy for organic assignment to hunter-killer units. Primarily, though, they will be used to permit a unit to remain on active patrol duty for a much longer period than would be the case if it were restricted to operating on the material resources that it could carry itself. Depending on the terrain, a patrol unit is normally restricted to four or five days of operations if it is solely dependent upon its self-carried supplies.

Using the Malayan Emergency again as an historical example, troop lifting, casualty evacuation, and supply dropping combined to multiply the number of troops deployed on productive anti-insurgent patrols by a factor of not less than four.[10] The probabilities for effective engagement and defeat of the guerrillas are considerably increased through the use of aerial transports.

Airborne Assault Operations—This aspect of airpower is generally accepted as being most important in counterinsurgency operations. It has already been noted several times that intelligence is a principal guerrilla strength. This intelligence normally travels by runner or bicycle or perhaps even by dugout canoe. These modes of transmission are more than satisfactory for reporting general preparation and march progress of advancing government troops. They are less satisfactory for motorized advances, but even in these cases the problem of mine-detection scrutiny ahead of the column forces it to move only slightly faster than foot troops. The methods of communicating intelligence on airborne operations, however, are completely unsatisfactory. The quick-reaction and rapid air delivery time preclude the guerrilla intelligence system from providing early warning to its units that are about to be attacked. This is another example of how technology can be used to exploit a weakness (time of transmission) of a standard guerrilla strength (a vast, popularly based intelligence net).

Airborne assaults in counterinsurgency war will generally be used for rapid exploitation of target intelligence and for rescue and assist operations. In either case an alert force consisting of troop units and transport aircraft is needed. It must be recognized at the outset that the maintenance of such an alert force on other than a very modest scale will pose a great problem, for, as long as such a force remains uncommitted, the stand-by alert is an uneconomical use of trained troopers and especially of critical transport aircraft and their crews.[11]

Mobile reserve alert forces primarily responsible for providing defense support to beleaguered government-controlled villages should be maintained if at all possible. The achievement of the goal of expanded population control is heavily dependent on such units.

Airpower will be used for quick exploitation of targets of opportunity and for reinforcements of ground units in a tactically untenable position. Therefore, the exact status of aircraft availability must be considered as a command decision to be made at the highest level, based on the specific insurgency situation.[12] It is axiomatic, though, that whenever the situation permits the maintenance of such a combined alert force it should indeed be organized and placed on a ready around-the-clock status.

No attempt will be made here to argue the virtues and sins of helicopter assault versus fixed-wing transport assault by paratroopers. Both air assault systems have their strengths and weaknesses. During future counterinsurgency wars, however, internal and external politico-military considerations will most likely result in an amalgam of older-model fixed-wing transports maintained by the incumbent's forces and foreign-supplied helicopters. Unless the foreign assistance is extensive, the fixed-wing aircraft will probably dominate and so will paratroop operations. Be this as it may, the important point to be made here is that, regardless of the specific mode of air assault, airborne operations can contribute greatly toward the achievement of the government's goal to engage and defeat the guerrilla forces.

It can be seen at this juncture that airpower in its various forms can indeed make a significant and substantial contribution toward an incumbent government's achievement of its three strategic objectives. It can provide this government with intelligence when all other sources appear closed, and it can deny the enemy the effective utilization of his abundant information relating to counterinsurgent operations. It can project the government's presence and its military strength to the far corners of the country. It can provide quick reaction to all sorts of emergency assistance requests from the villages. It can restore a balance in terms of capabilities for surprise possessed by the opposing forces, and then, employed with imagination, it can give the counterinsurgents the mobility and flexibility needed to assume the offensive. In total, airpower can provide an incumbent regime with a substantial and even a decisive supporting contribution toward victory against active Communist insurgency.

It must be appreciated at this juncture, however, that to derive maximum benefit from the use of airpower in intermediate phase insurgency, its operations must be closely coordinated with surface operations. Equally important, if indeed not more important—given the highly political nature of insurgency—is the need for extremely close military and civil cooperation and coordination in virtually all counterguerrilla actions. Proper organization of the counterinsurgency establishment is, of course, the key to the solution to this problem.

Civil and Paramilitary Organization

Since the control of the populace is the key objective for both counterinsurgents and insurgents, it follows that the incumbent government must get as many people involved in support of its reforms as is possible. It also follows as a consequence that the civil branches of government become directly involved in the conflict. Paramilitary forces and Emergency Councils appears to be organizational answers to these two objectives.

A council can be established at the national level and should consist of the cabinet membership plus the military chiefs of the national services under the directorship of the Head of Government. The standard composition of the councils below this level should include the chief civil administrator, the head of the paramilitary forces, the director of police, the commander (or his representative—usually a civil-affairs staff officer) of the regular military forces assigned within the particular administrative unit, and all other civil officials who can make a contribution to counterinsurgency operations (for example, directors of public information, transportation, and public works). Each council, under the directorship of its chief civil administrator, will coordinate all internal civil activities toward the common goal of defeating the insurgency. More important, it can insure the coordination of military activities with civil and paramilitary operations within the areas of joint responsibility. In short, below the national level these councils will be essentially decision-implementing and coordinating bodies. They must, nevertheless, be delegated sufficient decision-making authority to permit them to handle local tactical matters expeditiously.

The military commander will not, except at the national level, be subordinate to the civil head of his particular council, and, because of security reasons, he will seldom be able to disclose to this civilian his particular operations plans until the last possible moment. The civilian council members must appreciate the necessity for such restrictive actions on the part of their military colleague. The military commander, however, should also appreciate the necessities of taking the council's known, general views and the dispositions and capabilities of local paramilitary units into full consideration in the design of his plans.

The paramilitary forces will be of greatest benefit to the regular military establishment if they are organized at two different levels, provincial and local. The rationale for these forces, of course, is their replacement of regular troops on defensive assignments in rear areas so that the latter can be more fully utilized in mobile reserve defense units and in offensive patrol and interdiction operations.

There will often be a tendency within the regular military ranks to provide these paramilitary units with barely usable old equipment and little meaningful training. This erroneous concept among the professionals of the importance and the value of these citizen soldiers and their consequent actions must be changed. A counterinsurgency war may well have its major battles fought by these nonprofessionals. Lieutenant Colonel F. K. Kleinman (contributing editor, *Army*), upon concluding an inspection trip to the Republic of Vietnam in mid-1962, stated:

Everyone agrees that this war will be won at the village level. So the real hero is the civil guardsman (provincial militia like our state militia was originally) and the Self Defense Corpsman (village militia). In recent months, they have been holding off company and battalion size attacks despite heavy casualties. One force of 24 men fought for two hours until all were killed or

wounded. Another held off a full-scale attack until airborne (helicopter) regular reinforcements could arrive. They are fighting
every week. Unlike the regular units, whom the Viet Cong usually
avoid, Civil Guardsmen and Self Defense Corpsmen often meet
the enemy in pitched battles.[13]

Military Organization

Ground Forces—A military structure reflecting hierarchic
levels of command that are parallel to the civil administrative
establishment appears to be most desirable. For example,
corps areas and provinces and division areas and districts can
correspond in the government-secured areas. This parallel and
collocational military-civil organization will not only aid coordination within a particular area but also facilitate inter-area
coordination. Each military command headquarters element
down to battalion level should, where possible, have a civil
affairs staff officer billet. This man, trained in such coordina-
tional matters, can be the military commander's principal
instrument of contact with civil authorities.

Unfortunately, this organizational blueprint will not eliminate a problem that will undoubtedly characterize many
developing areas in times of insurgency. The national government, feeling somewhat insecure because of this overt threat
to its authority, will tend to overcentralize decision-making. It
will inhibit, or preclude by dictate, lateral communications
among provinces; some provincial chiefs may similarly preclude lateral communications among districts. Hence a request
for aid from a beleaguered military patrol or a besieged village
will have to go up the vertical chain of command before
assistance will be authorized by the provincial level or, if
interprovincial aid is required, by the national level. If communications are poor, an inordinate amount of time will be
consumed while this request is being duly processed. As was
the tragic case in South Vietnam during the late 1950's and

early 1960's, the relief forces often arrived too late to be of
any assistance to their dead countrymen.

As a minimum, excellent radio communications are called
for among all elements in the vertical chain of authority in
order to permit rapid transmission and timely high-command
reaction to such requests. Most important, lateral communications among provinces and districts and their counterpart
military headquarters must be authorized for all emergency
assistance requests to insure that the concept of rapid mutual
support can be meaningfully employed.

Air Forces—In prescribing organizational doctrine for a
developing state's air forces, it must be remembered that
Phase Two and Phase Three Communist insurgency warfare
will be marked by well-dispersed small- or medium-scale guerrilla operations. In most insurgency-beset nations, even those
with substantial foreign assistance, airpower will be a critical
and limited resource. Therefore, those air units that can furnish close air support, interdiction, photo reconnaissance, and
large-scale strategic airborne assault missions to ground forces
should not be made organic to these latter-type operational
commands. The flexibility of these units and the versatility,
range, and limited quantities of the aircrafts dictate that these
air weapon-systems be placed under the centralized control of
a joint operations center (JOC).

Within a JOC—which will contain current information on
the deployment and operations of all friendly units and a current intelligence display of all known enemy forces and
activities—air and ground officers and, when appropriate,
airborne forces' officers, can jointly evaluate all requests for
tactical air support or large-scale airborne operations. Their
response will be the product of their professional expertise
and their knowledge of the "big picture" situation which is
constantly before them. They will be in a position realistically
to assign priorities to each request for immediate and pre-
planned support operations and to select the specific air units

for carrying out prescribed action. Thus they will insure that in every support action the limited resource of airpower is most efficiently utilized.

The British were quite successful in employing centrally controlled airpower in their operations against the MRLA in Malaya. Conversely, French failures effectively to employ their airpower against the Vietminh under a system of decentralized airpower (in which air units were essentially organic to ground field forces) should also be noted, the lack of available air facilities notwithstanding.

Centralized air control and decentralized ground operations will obviously cause some coordination problems when such a composite system is first inaugurated. Essentially, this problem will relate to the absence of airpower expertise at the field operational levels to assist in the planning and decision-making relevant to air operations once a particular plan is implemented. To solve this problem, air support operations officers can be assigned to corps headquarters to assist in the preparations for large-scale operations and to process and evaluate requests for air support from lower-echelon field units.

In reviewing this brief section on civil-military organization, it is apparent that a great deal of coordination must exist between the mobilized civilian and the military components of a nation's popularly based and virtually all-encompassing counterinsurgency-force structure. Decentralized control of ground forces appears to be a necessary organizational precept whereas, conversely, it is equally imperative that the tactical air forces, including the airborne assault units, be organized so that control is fully centralized.

The three principal objectives of counterinsurgency operations—expansion of control over the populace, weakening and exposure of the insurgent bands, and engagement and defeat of the guerrilla forces—are inextricably interwoven. They must be pursued simultaneously at the strategic level

and, to a slightly lesser degree, at the tactical level as well.
Early emphasis in a particular campaign will have to be placed
on the achievement of the first two objectives so that the defeat of the guerrillas in the field will be facilitated.

Given these objectives and the nature of Communist insurgency warfare in its intermediate stages of development,
counterinsurgency planners and operational commanders can
so order and orient their endeavors and employ their available
resources as to bring a systematic and efficient approach to
the defeat of guerrilla forces.

The model of Communist insurgency warfare suggests,
however, that this conflict will not automatically be terminated
because the insurgent guerrillas have been beaten in military
combat. The Maoist concept of "revolutionary flow" anticipates
phases of an insurgency's development and prescribes that the
insurgency then revert back to Phase One operations.

7

The Noncombat Role
of the Military

The pervasive desires, if not demands, of the general populace for security and order during the periods of guerrilla actions in Phase Two or Phase Three Communist insurgency can often lead an incumbent regime into making a serious policy error once peace has been restored. With this military victory and the providing of protection to the outlying areas (by means of the fortification and resettlement projects) as well as the introduction of modest socioeconomic reforms (in pursuit of population control), the government may conclude that its defeat of the insurgency has been decisive. Such a conclusion can prove to be disastrous.

In addition to appreciating the consequences of the Maoist dictum of "revolutionary flow," the incumbent government cannot overlook the fact that the general populace's preoccupation with matters of security and order is explicitly a function only of the military actions of the opposing forces during intermediate phase insurgency operations. The regime must appreciate that the fundamental problem is the removal of socioeconomic and political inequities and the grievances that initially contributed to the development of internal wars. Subsequent to successful campaigns against the guerrillas in the field, the government must assume that a Phase One threat is

136

still present. It must organize and employ its resources to eliminate this threat so that the victory over Communist insurgency will be meaningfully consolidated.

Of course, the Phase One threat is present in virtually all developing states as the preparatory aspect of the cellular development of Communist insurgency warfare. Even though this and the situation above are obviously somewhat different, the prescriptive therapy in each case is quite similar. In this latter case these therapeutic actions can constitute a "preventive medicine" program; in both cases the goal is the elimination or at least the significant attenuation of the disruptive factors of instability that tend to breed insurgency.

One of two interconnected and composite objectives related to the achievement of this goal—which essentially calls for substantial increases in popular allegiance to the incumbent regime—is the breaking down of provincial and communal barriers and the incorporation of all groups, all peoples, all sections of a country into a national whole controlled by a respected central government. The other is the instituting of broad-scale development and reform programs in the socioeconomic and political areas of national life.

While these objectives have high priority for the civil components of a national government, a most significant role can be played by the indigenous military establishment. In addition to providing comprehensive back-up in depth to the civil police for the maintenance of internal order—which is essential for effective domestic reform and development operations and for the attraction of private, foreign investments—the military can contribute directly to the implementation of these programs. In many cases it may be better prepared than civilian agencies in terms of total resources, matériel, and personnel. This does not imply, however, that the armed forces should control the development programs. As was the case in the government's operations to meet and defeat intermediate phase insurgency, an effective response to Phase One requires extensive coordination of civil and military activities at virtually all levels of national administration. It is absolutely essential that these two components of the government integrate their operations so that each complements the other while both remain conscious of the fact that they are waging a "war" that is fundamentally political in nature.[1]

Much research has been undertaken in the area of the civil aspects of achieving reform and development. Recently, however, scholars specializing in the problems of underdevelopment have evidenced an increasing appreciation of the indigenous military establishments to the orderly process of political and economic modernization.[2] It is to this particular subject that this chapter will be addressed.

The military contribution to nation-building is generally referred to in Western military literature as *"military-civic action."* This term is defined as "any action which makes the soldier a brother of the people as well as their defender."[3] It can range upward from "basic individual acts of courtesy to disaster relief to local assistance programs up to major engineering projects."[4]

The military-civic action concept was part of the six-element plan for village fortification operations and of the prescribed resettlement programs designed to promote the government's objectives of expanding its control over the populace in the face of Phase Two or Phase Three insurgency. The nature and number of military-supported development and reform projects at such times, however, are limited by the high demands for personnel and material resources created by the government's active combat campaigns against the guerrillas. It is also quite conceivable that a particular state may be faced with multiple-phase insurgency. In other words, certain areas may be in Phase One while others may be experiencing intermediate phase Communist operations. In such cases it will obviously be inappropriate and even dangerous to devote extensive military resources to nation-building projects. In those situations, however, where the Phase One threat is exclusive or demonstrably dominant, such limitations will be substantially reduced if not altogether eliminated.

An incumbent regime—whether it has already experienced

guerrilla insurgency warfare or whether it is responding to anticipated domestic violence that it expects as a natural by-product of the development process—is normally compelled to maintain sizable armed forces to meet internal requirements. Some of these states may also be committed to defense pacts which require them to have large military establishments. Even with substantial foreign assistance for the military, a developing state can ill afford to tie up its technically trained personnel and material resources in such a manner when it is faced with pressing economic problems. A solution to this dilemma, therefore, appears to be the utilization of the military forces-in-being for projects related to a nation's socioeconomic and political development.

It is necessary to note at the very outset that the utilization of this resource for socioeconomic development may bring about liabilities that far exceed derived assets and benefits. For example, such military-civic action operations, if not properly designed and controlled, can possibly promote the establishment of military oligarchies. They may even stifle the creation and growth of civilian business enterprises essential to the development of viable economic and political institutions. These and other liabilities, as well as suggested methods for avoiding such problems, will be covered at greater length in the later sections of this chapter.

The following prescriptions are in essence a description of ideal rather than actual or automatic situations. With further research, it may prove possible to modify these prescriptions so that they will offer a high probability of success with none of the undesirable side effects.

The Military as a Resource for National Development

Many military leaders in the underdeveloped states were trained in the West or under a system of Western military tutelage in their own states. Consequently, there is a marked affinity among segments of this officer corps for the West or at least for their Western comrades under arms. These officers and the men they command are usually anti-Communist in basic political orientation. More important, the military establishment in most developing nations (with only a few exceptions among high-ranking officers in some Latin American states) tends to emphasize a rational outlook on life and to promote responsible change and national development.[5]

The reason is that these armies have been trained and equipped by the great industrial powers of the West. These indigenous military structures represent, historically speaking, the peculiar product of the most highly industrialized civilizations yet developed. As a consequence these establishments are generally imbued with a spirit that is tied to rapid technological development.[6] In a sense they often represent islands of modernity in the troubled seas of preindustrial societies striving for modernity.

A particularly significant dimension of this composite military resource is its technical and administrative expertise. These establishments have staff positions and related departments which call for skills that are in very short supply in their societies. Besides the more traditional service and support elements of engineers, signal corps, and medical corps, they contain transportation corps and chemical warfare, psychological warfare, personnel, finance, and matériel-procurement sections patterned after their Western counterparts. Many officers assigned to these specialized roles have received their advanced training in foreign military and civilian institutions. However, virtually all of these indigenous military establishments also operate, with foreign assistance, their own specialized technical training schools for junior officers and enlisted personnel. This military technical expertise, when combined with the equipment assigned especially to engineer, communications, transportation, and medical units, can play a vital role in a nation's quest for modernity.

Other significant dimensions of this general resource relate to the normal tactical dispersion of armed force units throughout the state during periods of peace. In many developing nations the government's presence in the outlying areas is maintained exclusively by soldiers assigned to outpost garrison duties. Through discipline, communications, and proper organization, these dispersed units are integrated into the national whole and are controlled through a chain of command by responsible decision-making personnel at the seat of the central government. This suggests that the military can be not only a primary agency in outlying local village development projects but also an important hub in any large-scale regional or national programs requiring extensive coordination plus adherence to directives from higher authority.

Finally, two other dimensions worthy of note relate to the general populace's view of the military. In many developing states the army represents the spirit of independence, the idea of national self-respect. Cultures that looked down upon their military establishments prior to the modernization of these forces now tend to give high respect to these agencies precisely because they have become so much more technologically advanced than their indigenous environs.[7]

Because of its progressive attitude toward the pursuit of modernity, its technical and professional expertise and related equipments, its organization and its prestige, the military establishment of an emerging state seems to possess a great potential that can be tapped by a government for constructive nation-building endeavors.

Public Works and Infrastructure Construction Programs

Community Construction Programs—These programs can normally be carried out on a part-time basis by garrison troops stationed at outposts throughout the countryside during periods of peace. In those nations that have constructed fixed fortified bases (FFB's) in conjunction with an earlier campaign against insurgent guerrillas, the forces assigned to these installations can be similarly used for such community construction projects within their designated territories. Usually these programs will require little if any expertise and equipment in addition to that already possessed by the assigned military unit and the village receiving its aid.

These projects, if they are to impart proper basic values to the villagers, must be joint endeavors between the troops and the local inhabitants. The concept of self-help should be firmly but gently inculcated into the minds of the villagers. Where possible, projects can be selected by local village leaders in conjunction with, or assisted by, officers from the appropriate supporting garrisons. Perhaps in some cases higher military headquarters can create mobile support advisory teams to assist villagers and the local military commanders in plotting a development program. Every effort must be made to give the villagers and their leaders a sense of significant involvement in these planning and construction operations. Thus a sense of local civic pride can emerge, and local leaders can be "educated" concurrently with the construction of the material facilities to sustain the development processes of the community.

There are several other pertinent considerations. To insure a quick and meaningful impact upon the people—that is, to demonstrate quickly and positively the regime's determination to aid the villagers—initial projects for military-civic action should have short completion times. Results should be tangible, and end-products should lend themselves to easy publicity. This may well inspire other military units to emulate actions of those comrades engaged in such pursuits, and the local inhabitants will readily be able to associate derived benefits with the armed forces and the central government which these forces represent.[8]

These small-scale, joint actions can include the construction of irrigation and drainage systems, feeder roads to principal transportation lines, simple bridges, and various other local public-works facilities such as schools, central market-places, civic centers, grain storage buildings, potable water systems, and basic sewage disposal installations. Needless to say, while these projects are designed primarily for rural community development, similar endeavors can be launched by military units stationed in urban centers.

To be most effective, the city programs will have to be directed toward those sectors inhabited by the "floating masses" of unemployed who are recent emigrants from the agrarian countryside. Related projects can range from the simple construction of basic dwellings for destitute families—as was done, for example, by the Colombian Army's Ayacucha Brigade in the city of Belen de Umbria[9]—to more ambitious urban cleanup campaigns and road construction programs such as those carried out by Burmese Army garrison units in Rangoon.[10]

Infrastructure Construction Programs—These large-scale projects will have to be carried out by specialized military units, such as engineer construction battalions (ECB's), possessing high-level professional and technical skills and substantial amounts of heavy equipment. Normally, the number of such units in an emerging country will be severely limited, and the resources needed for their sustained operations will be considerable. However, the value of their specialized training will significantly enhance the general capabilities of the national military forces. The value of the end-products of such training operations (various infrastructure facilities) is virtually inestimable to a nation striving to develop into a modern politico-economic entity. The dictates of efficiency, economy, and military security combine to suggest that such construction units be used to their maximum capability.

Logical infrastructure end-products for ECB training exercises are large bridges, railroads, canals, air facilities, ports, communications systems, and power and sanitation projects. Priority construction targets can be prescribed by the civilian agencies of the government responsible for economic development. Although the number of such large-scale construction endeavors in underdeveloped states has been limited, it is significant that those completed have been fairly successful. Paraguayan and Peruvian national roads have been built under this operation as have air facilities in Bolivia, Honduras, and Ethiopia.

Socioeconomic Services Programs

Education—The military establishment of a developing state can also assist the government in spreading education throughout the nation. In addition to educating its own personnel, it can provide basic education for village inhabitants in the more remote areas.

It is a generally accepted fact that armies are supposed to make civilian recruits into professional soldiers. As Lucian Pye has pointed out, however, in underdeveloped nations there is the added dimension that the good soldier be also to some degree the modernized man.[11] An indigenous military establishment thereby expedites the acculturative process through which the traditional dimensions of a society give way to more Westernized ideas and modes of social existence.

Probably the most significant feature of this acculturation process—since it takes place within a highly organized and integrated military establishment—is that it provides a relatively high degree of psychological security to the new recruit.[12] His experience, although obviously somewhat traumatic, is not too disruptive of his general emotional behavior because his exposure to the complexities of modernity is generally graduated and prescriptively controlled. This is not usually the case for his rural counterpart who migrates to the city and, in the process of his personal urbanization, becomes an insecure, restless, and volatile individual susceptible to exploitation by extremists and purveyors of violence.

The focus of the acculturative process is the acquisition

of literacy and technical capabilities. These skills, when combined with the serviceman's new understanding and appreciation of the value of modern communications and transportation, of sanitation and health, and, above all, of Western concepts of organization and planning, contribute toward making this individual a significant asset to a developing state. He is such whether he remains within the military or is discharged and assumes his role in civilian life as a personal expediter and a catalyzing agent of socioeconomic progress.

The military establishment usually provides its members with a limited sociopolitical education. The men are compelled to broaden their horizons and to see themselves and their brothers under arms—who come from various sections of the country—as parts of a large national whole. This experience generally instills in these men a sense of patriotism. Significantly, it also forces them to re-evaluate their ideas about destiny. They become aware that human decisions rather than fate determine most experiences in social existence. Fundamentally, these educational experiences not only tie the individual to his state but also make him a politically conscious individual.[13] He thus becomes potentially capable of making significant contributions to the reform and development programs of his government.

It is quite evident that the armed forces in an emerging state, through their internal educational programs, provide their nation not only with an indigenous military competence to handle modern conventional weapons, but also with a reservoir of acculturated, technically trained personnel who have a reasonably good potential for becoming politically responsive and responsible citizens. This, however, is only part of their contribution to a national program of education.

These trained personnel can also serve as teachers in the remote settlements which do not attract civilian educators. The military garrison units can not only assist the villagers in the construction of their schools but also staff these elementary institutions once they are completed. Thus they can supply the villagers with educational services until civilian education agencies assume this task. Such programs in Burma and Turkey have been marked with considerable success.

Another way in which the military can service the educational requirements of outlying villages is through aerial television transmitting programs or through the less technically demanding and extensively tried and proved method of education via radio. In a nonmilitary program conducted by the American Foundation of Cultural Popular Action, Inc., for the remote regions of Colombia, over 700,000 peasants have been taught the proverbial three "R's," agricultural methods, hygiene, nutrition, and sports over a twelve-year period.[14] Military personnel assigned to remote regions can be made responsible for the maintenance of village receiving sets and can provide technical tutoring to supplement the radio presentations.

Agriculture—The military can support agricultural programs through education services programs, and construction projects to prevent floods and to permit timely irrigation of farm plots. In addition to this, it can employ its garrison troops for land-clearing projects and for the preliminary agricultural development of virgin lands. Israel's novel system of "constructive idealism," for example, as applied to military support for national agriculture development requires that most two-year conscripts be given basic military training coupled with extensive on-the-job agricultural training in the frontier regions. Service aircraft can be employed in crop-dusting operations. With the use of the military's communications net and its meteorological services, pertinent weather information can be transmitted throughout the countryside. When harvesting crash programs are needed because of forecasts of seriously adverse weather conditions, the military garrison units should assist the peasants.

Public Health—In this area, too, the military can complement its projects and services to promote public health and sanitation programs. It can employ its aircraft in spray missions designed to eliminate disease-bearing insects. Military air or surface transport vehicles can be used for the emergency evacuation of critically injured or seriously ill village inhabitants in the remote regions. Military personnel assigned to garrison duties in the outlying areas can implement inoculation programs. They can also provide, on a regularly scheduled basis, "circuit rider" medical service to all isolated villages. Military personnel can also provide technical advice and can transport necessary materials for comprehensive pest-control and fertilizing programs.

Transportation—Indigenous, private-enterprise transportation organizations in the more remote areas usually do not have either the economic or the technological capability to support sustained operations on a profitable basis. The indigenous air force or navy can be called upon by the government to promote political control and socioeconomic development.

Public Administration

Efficient public administration is essential for an orderly and progressive development of emerging states to modernity. Authority should be regulated and predictable, and its executors should possess substantive and procedural expertise. Unfortunately, many civil sectors of government will not have sufficient trained personnel to fill all required positions. The military establishment may be able somewhat to fill this void on a temporary basis. Military and noncommissioned officers (NCO's) can be assigned to civil administrative positions at national and provincial levels of government.

It must be emphasized that these assignments are to be temporary and more administrative than political in character. To preserve and promote the concept of civil primacy during the military officer's tenure, he must be directly subordinate to higher civil authority and should be replaced as soon as a competent civilian administrator can be trained.

The temptation of higher civil authority to retain the efficient, well-organized, and highly patriotic military personnel in such offices for long durations will be natural and great. Such temptation must be resisted if a healthy representative polity is to emerge together with the evolution of a modern nation-state.

The dangers of prolonged military participation in public administration revolve around the problem of criticism. Military officers and NCO's will be unable to accept criticism to the same degree as their civilian counterparts. This stems from the simple fact that this type of relationship with subordinates or with the general receivers of professional services does not characterize military operations. The result is that there may well be little opportunity for the satisfactory solving of essential conflicts of interests within certain affected segments of a national society. Political criticism can thus very well be stifled as an end-product of such a state of affairs. The opportunities to develop an open and viable political system may therefore be unintentionally foreclosed. The Burmese experience may be particularly instructive in this regard.[15]

By focusing attention on levels of government below the national and provincial levels, one can see great opportunities to utilize the military's administrative expertise, which is resident in the remote garrison posts or the FFB's, to service the requirements of the outlying villages. In addition to assisting in community development projects associated with construction programs and providing various socioeconomic services, military personnel can aid village councils in the establishment and operation of an efficient local bureaucratic structure. Assistance will include advice and instruction in such matters as census taking; maintenance of records on vital community data (births, deaths, educational information); proper conduct of meetings so that they can be most productive and rewarding to all concerned; basic problem-solving and phase-planning techniques; and the procedural and clerical functions that normally mark local administration. It is interesting that the Filipino Armed Forces, under orders from Magsaysay, actually employed judge advocate officers as lawyers to represent poor peasants in their legal actions against land owners.[16]

Here again, however, to be most effective in long-range goals, this assistance must be only of a temporary nature. It must focus upon on-the-job training and then upon withdrawal of the instructor at the earliest conceivable time. If at all possible, a joint project between locally assigned military units and civil training cadres from the central or provincial governments seems to be called for. Such cadres, developed along the lines of the Filipino Community Development Teams or the Vietnamese Civic Action Teams, can first assist the military and ultimately replace it in such operations. For those nations beset with the problem of unemployed loyal intellectuals, these civilian civic action teams (and even similar military teams) can be staffed by college graduates who need a challenge and a meaningful and constructive mission in life. Until the creation of such teams, this burden will continue to fall upon military units.

It is important to remember that these representatives of the central government, whether they be military or civilian, are merely fulfilling training and advisory functions. To carry out properly their particular contribution to nation-building, they cannot ordinarily assume direct responsibility for the civil-administrative functions of the settlements. While these experts are supposed to promote a gravitation of the villages toward the central government, it is important that they cultivate a free and open political communion between local leaders and the officials of higher levels of government. Also, they must inculcate into their students the fundamentals of viable, representative, local governance. In so doing, they will be setting the foundations for long-term political stability.

It is reasonable to assume that these particular training operations will lead to the emergence of political leadership

and sophistication at the grass-roots level; they also can ultimately lead to a diffusion of the newly found strength as well
as the power of the central government throughout the national whole. This is apparently the core element of the Filipino
national government's *Barrio Charter* and also possibly of the
Basic Democracies program of Pakistan's President Ayub
Khan. As Professor Frank Tannenbaum has stated:

> If anything definite can be said about political revolutions, it
> is that they do not and cannot take place in countries where
> political strength is dispersed in a thousand places, and where
> myriads of men feel personally involved in the continuing prob-
> lems of a self-governing parish or township and participate in
> making the rules for the larger unit, county, state or nation.[17]

Before we turn to a cost and gains analysis of military-
civic action operations, we must note that the scope and depth
of these activities can be considerably increased if foreign aid
—monetary, technical, and material—is received by the local
armed forces. This can range from purely specialized assistance, such as "Operation Brotherhood," the Filipino contribution of civilian medical teams to assist the Republic of
Vietnam's civic-action program, to comprehensive technical
and extensive material aid, both civil and military, such as
has been given by the United States to the Republic of Korea
in its civic-action operations.

Problems and Prospects of Military-Civic Action Operations

Positive Aspects—A developing state benefits greatly by
utilizing its armed forces for civic-action programs. The military establishment can serve as an acculturating and educating vehicle for thousands of the nation's youth. It can provide
the state with internal security during the critical and sensi-
tive periods of reform and development; at the same time it
can contribute technically trained, nationalistically oriented,

and, possibly, politically conscious manpower to the civilian
sector of the nation. It can break down provincial barriers
and develop educational and basic socioeconomic programs in
the outlying areas, thus bringing the national government
and the benefits of the modernized sectors of the economy
to all the people.

The armed forces can construct vital infrastructure facilities and provide the communications and transportation services essential for economic development. They can introduce
the concepts of organization, discipline, and efficiency into
civil governance and improve administration from the national
down to the local village levels.

These advances will occur mainly through the utilization
of existing resources and not by the creation of new agencies
and the acquisition of additional resources. The costs, therefore, can be considered within reasonable bounds by a central
government working with limited amounts of trained personnel and capital. Of course, all these operations tend to eradicate or weaken those factors of instability that breed Phase
One Communist insurgency.

If insurgency does break out after such programs have
been initiated—perhaps in response to their initial successes
—the good will previously generated among the peasants
will make the guerrillas' task of securing intelligence and of
finding safety among the populace very difficult. Also, the
construction of infrastructure facilities will facilitate the
government's job of bringing superior weapons to bear directly
upon the enemy's field forces. Many military authorities con-
tend that the very absence of such facilities in Laos contributed greatly to the inability of the Laotian Army to defeat
the Pathet Lao guerrilla forces.

As is the case with most apparently appealing solutions
to a complex problem, there are many liabilities as well as
assets associated with military-civic action operations.

Negative Aspects—The official promotion of military operations into areas traditionally reserved for civilian enterprise

can pose many problems and threats to an orderly political development for an emerging state pursuing rapid socioeconomic progress. The inherent instability naturally creates among the citizenry psychological conditions conducive to giving political power to the military, which is often the only organization having effective force, organization, and discipline. Is it wise, therefore, for a civil government voluntarily to transfer extensive economic and political responsibilities to the military under such conditions? The answer appears to be No if such action will ultimately cause a diminution of civil power and the *de facto* assumption of principal, national, and political power by the armed forces.

If the traditions of civil primacy are not strong, if few democratic values are firmly established, and if national life could be marked with some long-term instability incident to the developmental processes, then control by the military would also become a long-term phenomenon. History is full of cases in which military regimes—however altruistically motivated they may have been—have ended up, after an extended period of rule, stifling the give-and-take political processes essential to an efficient and sound civil government. It is true that similar situations can develop under essentially civilian control, but the assumption of such comprehensive powers by the military is especially laden with long-term trouble.

The recorded past is replete with examples which strongly suggest that military government is somewhat similar to malaria. Once the military has tasted the complete powers of government and then relinquished them either voluntarily or otherwise, its seat offstage appears to be an uncomfortable one. It remains as an alternative to civil government. To the masses it can be called back to over-all power in a chaotic situation; to the military hierarchy it is available to "save" the nation from the "corrupt and disruptive" practices of political parties or "unpatriotic and self-seeking" civilian political leaders. The histories of many Latin American states and the recent experiences in Burma appear partially to substantiate this contention.

A consequence of military control can be the creation of a military-oriented hypernationalism among the general populace. This in turn would lead to the continued presence of exceptionally large military establishments and could contribute to the state's pursuit of opportunistic and offensive foreign policies that could disrupt and exacerbate existing East-West tensions.

Even if political power is not a problem, the construction and socioeconomic service projects undertaken by the military can adversely affect both the capital-management and the organized labor sectors of a national economy. This could easily discourage free enterprise projects that stimulate the economy. The Argentine experience is instructive here: in 1962, the Army owned the largest national industrial empire. Or, organized labor may view troop labor as unfair competition in a market characterized by limited unskilled and semi-skilled job opportunities.

Reversing the focus, extensive military-civic action operations by other than engineer construction battalions—and even possibly these units in certain circumstances—may cause armed forces personnel to lose their proficiencies for combat actions. Any long-term commitments of regular units to projects requiring troop labor activities could lead to a general and fundamental deterioration of troop morale. Both situations can produce a drastic decline in the combat effectiveness of a military establishment—for both internal and interstate war.

Balance—The above cost-and-gains analysis indicates that developing states should not plunge headlong into military-civic action projects without carefully evaluating each activity in a broad sociopolitical and military context. Under virtually no circumstances should the civil authorities abdicate their legal sovereignty in favor of political control of the state by the military establishment. Neither should military leaders, as they become impatient with the imperfections of civil governance, lose sight of the fact that once they assume full powers—even if only temporarily—they have established a dangerous and lasting precedent.

No projects should be undertaken by the military that in any way will directly compete with and possibly discourage, if not destroy, the initiation of indigenous free-enterprise operations, nor should the military be assigned civic action tasks if civil-public agencies exist with the capabilities of carrying out these operations.

Finally, absolutely no long-term civic-action projects should be undertaken that will seriously interfere with necessary training programs and thus erode the fighting effectiveness of the military establishment.

In concluding this chapter it must be re-emphasized that there are no easy and automatic solutions to the problems of socioeconomic and political modernization. The aforementioned prescriptions obviously do not constitute a panacea for all the ills of underdevelopment. But it is equally obvious that most emerging states have made little effort to harness the potential of their military establishments for nation-building programs. However, given the imperatives of reform and development and the nature of Phase One Communist insurgency, it appears that affected states should permit their armed forces, under carefully supervised civil control, to approach their maximum constructive role in the modernization process.

PART THREE

A Proposal for
an American Response

8

An American Counterinsurgency Establishment

The preceding chapters have dealt almost exclusively with incumbent regime responses to Communist-initiated insurgency warfare. Implicit in this emphasis on the role of local forces is the contention that counterinsurgency operations must be overwhelmingly dominated by indigenous government elements if they are to succeed.

Excessive external assistance to an emerging nation, especially if marked by the presence of a great number of foreign personnel, can well raise the specter of a "new colonialism" in the eyes of the local populace. Lieutenant Colonel Villa-Real, a counterinsurgency specialist of the Philippine Armed Forces, has stated:

> Foreign troops are certain to be less welcome among the people than are the regular armed forces of their own government. Local populations will shelter their own people against operations of foreign troops, even though those they shelter may be outlaws. For this reason, native troops would be more effective than foreign forces in operations against native communist conspirators. It would be rare, indeed, if the use of foreign troops would not in itself doom to failure an anti-guerrilla campaign.[1]

Nevertheless, most insurgency-besieged developing states will require some outside help if they are to defeat Communist insurgency in the shortest possible time. The United States, as the leader of the Free World, must assume the principal responsibility for providing such aid. Its actions can run the gamut of assistance operations.

Diplomatic support, economic aid, and military assistance are available alternatives. In a few exceptional cases, the United States may be compelled to employ American forces in a limited and temporary manner directly to support local counterinsurgents. With the possible exception of diplomatic support, the United States must maintain a background position in these activities. The benefits of such support, as viewed by the indigenous populace, must be transformed into credits first for the incumbent government and then for the United States.

To be effective, the organization's design and subsequent operations must reflect two considerations: the nature of the problem itself and the availability of resources. American counterinsurgency must overwhelmingly support operations, not combat insurgents.

It is important to review some American prejudices that must be submerged before an effective counterinsurgency support organization can be designed and set into operation. For example, the United States apparently can no longer afford to view aggression as something that is clear-cut and easily discernible even to the untrained eye. Neither can this nation continue to view victory as a climactic and total military triumph.

It has already been amply demonstrated that the psychopolitical mobilization of the people is the main objective of the opposing forces in an insurgency-counterinsurgency situation. As the battlegrounds will generally be located in the developing areas, a counterinsurgency campaign, to have reasonable chances for success, will have to encompass broad sociopolitical reform and economic development programs.

Even as they concern military operations *per se*, political factors will play an extremely important role in action from the national level right down to local field situations. Hence the American counterinsurgency-support establishment will have to supply across-the-board assistance to an incumbent regime, and the orientation of its operations will have to reflect the dominant role of the political factor in this type of internal war. This in turn will overcome the tendency to oversimplify and divide military and political activities into two largely separate and distinct spheres.

American tradition rightly raises a barrier that prohibits political activities by the uniformed services within the context of our own government. This barrier, however, should not preclude utilization of American military technical advisors in nonmilitary nation-building projects being carried out by the armies of the developing states. The American precedent for such activities is substantial and should not be overlooked. For example, the United States Army's Corps of Engineers and its companion service, the Corps of Topographical Engineers, completed numerous projects related to the exploitation of remote natural resource deposits and the construction of expansive infrastructure systems, and numerous public buildings (especially in the national capital). Other United States military agencies have played significant roles in providing medical, educational, logistic, and public administration services to the frontier regions as America developed into a modern, expansive, industrial power.

Neither should this barrier be used to preclude the transfer of development funds within a particular state from a United States civilian agency, which does not have the wherewithal for a particular project, to the resident American agency, which, because of its connection with the indigenous armed forces and its own organic expertise, can complete the required project by means of civic-action operations.

Still another conceptual problem concerns the element of time. Americans will have to overcome their natural inclina-

tion to view counterinsurgency warfare—as they have traditionally viewed all other forms of warfare—as a sort of foot-
ball game with a series of critical points, at no one of which
is a certain outcome foreseeable. More important, they will
have to correct their tendency to be excessively preoccupied
with promoting and practicing the principle of the economy
of time, an idea that seemingly dominates American military
and foreign-policy planning.[2]

Americans must finally learn the value of patience, which
should be the mark of a leader-state worthy of its important
position within the Free World. Communist insurgency warfare, once it reaches its second or third phase of development,
will be a long and costly affair and will not be subject to
immediate solution, regardless of how extensive American aid
is to an affected emerging nation. Together with patience
should come an appreciation for the value of long-term objectives. With these attributes American programs will be
more realistically designed; frustrations and resultant disrupt-
ing fluctuations of policy will be minimized, and the temptation to support regimes which adamantly refuse to meet the
genuine aspirations of their people will be considerably reduced.

After accepting W. W. Rostow's thesis—"the best way to
fight guerrilla war is to prevent it from happening"[3]—the
United States must modify even further its traditional doctrine of nonintervention in the internal affairs of foreign
states. The American government can provide strong incentives for regimes in the emerging states to take socioeconomic
and political measures that can significantly eliminate or
attenuate the local factors of instability and can promote
sound growth and development. The temptations of policy
makers, however, to avoid early political intervention are
usually strong in American decision-making circles. Indirect
political intervention is quite naturally difficult, complex, and
uncertain. Pressuring a friendly regime obviously appears less
palatable than taking direct action against common enemies.[4]

Yet apply pressure it must if the United States is to carry out
its responsibilities and fulfill its role as the leader-state of the
West.

The factors of time and intervention take on a new importance when viewed against the backdrop of the cellular
development of Communist insurgency warfare. It is obvious
that a direct relationship must exist between the prompt-
ness and the intensity of the response by an incumbent government challenged by this developing and expanding threat.
It is equally obvious that once such a government solicits appropriate assistance, the United States—if it desires to aid the
affected government—must respond in as expeditious a manner as is possible. Only in this way will early assistance help
to forestall the development of an insurgency. The fact that
this aid is directed against an early stage tends to insure that
the support need not be so expansive and all-encompassing
as to be genuinely unpalatable to the beleaguered incumbent
government. In terms of the medical analogy previously used,
the earlier that American assistance is effectively brought to
bear on the insurgent movement, the less extensive and in-
tensive will the over-all therapy have to be. Therefore, the
application of such treatment will be less painful to the patient (the emerging state).

The extent and intensiveness of this American aid may
be of direct concern to the United States in still another way.
The degree of American commitment and hence American
prestige involved in such operations will be a function of these
two qualitative and quantitative characteristics of assistance.
Even though the United States may have an obligation to
assist most friendly governments against internal Communist
insurgency, it obviously will not wish fully to commit its
prestige in each such support activity, especially if the incumbent regime is not sincerely attempting domestic socioeconomic reform and is despised by the populace at large.

The United States counterinsurgency-support establishment will therefore have to be designed so as to minimize

the extent and intensiveness of American assistance consistent with insuring meaningful victory to the counterinsurgent forces. It should be able to anticipate requests for counterinsurgency support so that, once the decision is made in Washington to render such assistance to a particular government, this aid can be delivered and effectively deployed in the most rapid manner possible.

A fundamental precondition for American intervention, of course, will be an invitation for such action from insurgency-affected governments. It is quite conceivable that, despite increasing evidence of rapidly developing Phase One and even Phase Two Communist insurgency, such governments will be reluctant to invite assistance. In many cases the United States may not be asked to intervene actively until an insurgency is well advanced into its intermediate phases. For this reason another design criterion is needed. The establishment should be able to handle the contingency of a late intervention and cope with all the logistics problems that will arise.

Finally, given the unconventional nature of guerrilla operations that mark intermediate phase insurgency, American military units assigned to this establishment will have to be specially educated and trained for this warfare. Then they will be able to instruct foreign military personnel in this unorthodox combat, and, should direct intervention be called for, the United States will have a force ready for this military operation.

The U.S. Armed Forces, therefore, must develop a doctrine and an operational capability to meet this threat in the same effective manner in which it has organized military establishments that continue to play a vital role in deterring potential aggressors from initiating general or limited wars against any member state of the Western Alliance. Fortunately, most of the components for such an enterprise exist at the time of this writing. The problem is essentially one of combining these elements into a specific mission-oriented and command-dominated operational structure. A survey of these components, most of them little known outside of government circles, is presented below.

Existing Organizational Resources

Interdepartmental Task Force—At the Washington level of command, the principal instrumentality available for counterinsurgency warfare direction and control is the *ad hoc* task force. This body is designed to meet a particular command requirement once an insurgency has developed or appears to be in the offing. The State Department provides the leadership for each body, and "desk officers," or area specialists—who represent those American governmental agencies having major responsibilities in the particular affected nation—fill out its membership.

The Country Team—By far the most important American contribution to an incumbent regime combating Phase One Communist insurgency will be made by the Country Team. Despite the great importance of the "Country Team," there is in fact very little that has been published on the subject. Yet through it the United States expends several billions of dollars annually in its Cold War operations, and it may well be the key to effective counterinsurgency operations in any given underdeveloped state.

The Country Team is not an agency or a command group with precise organizational structure. It seems to be essentially a technique or a concept of business management. As this concept has evolved, the chief of an American diplomatic mission has become the team leader and chief coordinator of *all* official United States agency activities in the state to which he is accredited. As team leader he has been given the responsibility by the President of the United States of carrying out the Country Plan, the policy prescribed from Washington for that particular nation.

The actual relationships between the ambassador and the

other resident American agency representatives are spelled out in the late President Kennedy's letter of May 29, 1961, to all American chiefs of diplomatic missions. This letter reads, in part, as follows:

> In regard to your personal authority and responsibility, I shall count on you to oversee and coordinate all the activities of the U.S. Government in ———.
>
> You are in charge of the entire U.S. diplomatic mission, and I shall expect you to supervise all of its obligations. The mission includes not only the personnel of the Department of State and the Foreign Service, but also the representatives of all other U.S. agencies which have programs or activities in ———. I shall give you full support and backing in carrying out your assignment.
>
> Needless to say, the representatives of other agencies are expected to communicate directly with their offices here in Washington, and in the event of a decision by you in which they do not concur, they may ask to have the decision reviewed by a higher authority in Washington.
>
> However, it is their responsibility to keep you fully informed of their views and activities and to abide by your decisions unless in some particular instance you and they are notified to the contrary.[5]

The composition of the Country Team will vary from nation to nation. Generally, the ambassador will serve as its head, and several key members of his own staff (the economic and political attaches, for example) will assist him. Membership will usually include the director of the Country Mission of the Agency for International Development (AID), the chief of the Military Assistance and Advisory Group (MAAG) or the chief of the Military Mission, the chief of the mission of the United States Information Agency, and other American agency heads or representatives deemed appropriate by the ambassador (for example, special United States Treasury representatives, Atomic Energy Commission representatives, and the like). Just as the composition of such a team will vary with the dictates of individual ambassadors, so the mode of operation will vary on a country-by-country basis. In some states the team will be simply an *ad hoc* body convened on certain occasions without a prescribed agenda. In other situations it may exist as a rather rigid and formal body that meets according to a set schedule to discuss items on a previously distributed agenda. In either case it can readily be seen that the Country Team concept is essentially a reversal of the normal post-World War II trend toward the ever increasing centralization of decision-making processes in Washington.

As a management technique, the Team can be used to restore necessary day-to-day and even person-to-person relationships within the general management framework of the official United States colony resident in a foreign state. It can insure that any composite American program for a particular state—whether it be simply an economic development project or a complex interagency endeavor to support the incumbent regime in its campaign against insurgency—will be effectively, efficiently, and expeditiously carried out in the best interests of the host nation and the United States.

*Military Assistance Advisory Group (MAAG) and Military Missions**—According to the Foreign Assistance Act of 1961, the Secretary of State, under the direction of the President, has over-all responsibility for the Military Assistance Program (MAP), of which the MAAG's are the principal operational instrumentalities. The Secretary of Defense is responsible for the implementation of those policies prescribed by the Secretary of State. In order to assure that various aid programs pursued by the Agency for International Development (AID) and by the Defense Department complement one another and directly contribute to the achievement of United States objectives, AID has a special staff responsible for performing the necessary, over-all coordination of these related activities.

Within the Department of Defense, the Joint Chiefs of Staff (JCS), the Assistant Secretary of Defense for International Security Affairs (ASD/ISA), and the military departments play major roles in the actual implementation of the

* Throughout this chapter the term MAAG will be used. However, the term *Military Mission* may be used in those cases where it is the principal if not the exclusive representative of the United States Department of Defense in a particular nation.

MAP. The last-mentioned organizations, of course, supply the trained personnel to the MAAG's and provide ASD/ISA with all technical and budgetary data relevant to the development and implementation of these programs. With approval of the Director of Military Assistance, the Departments sell military equipment and related services to eligible nations and provide the MAAG's and unified commands with technical military advice about weapon systems, tactics, and doctrine.

The next important organizational echelon is the regional unified command (similar to the "theater commands" of World War II). Here one senior American military officer, together with multiservice staff, is placed in charge of all military operations within an assigned geographic area. As they relate to military assistance activities, the pertinent commands are: US CINCSO (Commander-in-Chief, South), whose area of responsibility is all of Latin America; EUCOM (Commander-in-Chief, Europe), whose area of responsibility covers North Africa, the Near East, and South Asia (including Pakistan); PACOM (Commander-in-Chief, Pacific), whose area of responsibility includes the Far East and Southeast Asia. Tropical Africa, it should be noted, is not the responsibility of a unified command in regard to military assistance; the Department of the Army has direct control over the activities in this region.

These unified commands have substantial supervisory control over all the MAAG's assigned to nations within their geographic areas of responsibility. They provide an intermediate level of policy guidance and review between the Departments of State and Defense and the MAAG's. Thus country military assistance programs and activities are integrated on a regional basis before they are forwarded to Washington. As viewed by the chief of MAAG in a particular host nation, the unified commander is the only level of command between himself and the Assistant Secretary of Defense for International Security Affairs. As viewed by the latter, the unified command represents a regional "field office" for the execution of the national Military Assistance Program.

Finally, the MAAG itself, or in some cases the American Military Mission, must be described. In some states it will include three sections representing each of the major uniformed services. Other MAAG's may contain only one or two sections of the three that are called for in the Executive Agreement between the United States and the host country.

The chief of MAAG in a particular nation will almost always be an important member of the American ambassador's Country Team. With his service section heads, he is responsible for designing a Country Military Assistance Program based on general policy directives from ASD/ISA and the appropriate unified command. This program is first coordinated through the ambassador and the Country Team as a whole, then forwarded to the relevant unified command and ultimately to the Defense Department for review and approval. The final, reviewed, approved, and coordinated program is then sent back to the chief of MAAG for implementation, and this particular program becomes a part of the over-all Country Plan.

In the event of nonconcurrence by the ambassador on a part of the program and inability of the MAAG chief and the ambassador to resolve the difference, each submits his respective views and the problem is resolved at the Department of State-Department of Defense level in Washington. The specific duties of MAAG personnel to implement the program include training, advisory, and operational review functions. This aid, combined with war material from the United States, help to create a modernized and sophisticated indigenous military establishment. MAAG personnel may well become America's "front-line troops" if the nation to which they are accredited becomes involved in military operations against intermediate-phase Communist insurgency.

Strike Command (STRICOM)—The mission of this command was succinctly stated by Secretary of Defense Robert S. McNamara in a presentation to the Senate Armed Forces Committee on January 19, 1962:

> The recently created Strike Command—composed of units from the Strategic Army Corps and the Tactical Air Command—is intended to provide an integrated, mobile, highly combat-ready force which has trained as a unit and is instantly available for use and an augmentation to existing theater forces under the unified commanders, or as the primary force for use in remote areas such as Central Africa or the Middle East.[6]

This indeed is a unique military organization. Whereas it combines components from two services (Army and Air Force), it has no combat forces that are actually organic to it on a full-time basis. The Army component is made up of the combat-ready units in the United States Army's strategic reserve forces assigned to the Continental Army Command based in the United States. The Air Force component consists of fighter-bomber, reconnaissance, troop carrier, and aerial tanker squadrons that are integral parts of the United States Air Force's Tactical Air Command, which is also stationed in the continental United States. The commanders of these two major organizations have "second-hat" positions as the component commanders of STRICOM.

The forces assigned to these component commands and their respective commanders come under STRICOM control jurisdiction only during joint training exercises or during prescribed contingency missions as directed by the Secretary of Defense or the Joint Chiefs of Staff. STRICOM, through its special relationships with the single-manager transportation agencies service of the military forces, the Military Air Transport Service, the Military Sea Transportation Service, and the Defense Traffic Management Service assembles, moves, and delivers to regional unified commands forces that have trained together. Then these forces come under the operational control of the appropriate unified commander and are used to meet his contingency requirements.

The exception to this operational rule is related to contingency situations that may occur in sub-Saharan Africa or the Middle East. These cases call for the Commander of STRICOM directly to control units that have been taken from his component organization not only during assembly and transport to target areas but also during their commitment to action in accordance with orders from the JCS.

The unique capabilities of STRICOM for rapid deployment of combat-ready forces to any point on the globe tend to make obvious the utility of this command in the United States counterinsurgency establishment.

Specialized Units—Among these units the Special Forces Groups of the United States Army are particularly significant. According to the testimony of former Secretary of the Army Elvis Stahr, a detachment of such American forces consisting of ten enlisted personnel and two officers can effectively organize, control, and assist in the operations of a foreign guerrilla force of more than one thousand men.[7] Even though their primary orientation is in offensive guerrilla operations, this expertise, when combined with their secondary specialty, counterguerrilla warfare, and their extensive training and capability for sustained operations in hostile territory, make the Special Forces substantial assets to any United States counterinsurgency-support organization.

At the time of this writing, there are four United States Army Special Forces Groups. Two are assigned to the Special Warfare Center at Fort Bragg, North Carolina, and one each to Okinawa and Germany.

The United States Air Force has special airborne units created and trained specifically to cope with the problems of counterguerrilla warfare. The nucleus for these forces is the Special Air Warfare Center at Eglin Air Force Base, Florida. This center has assigned to it the 1st Air Commando Group and the Combat Applications Group. The former consists of squadrons made up of propeller and early subsonic-jet aircraft that dominate the air-order-of-battle of most developing nations. In the words of General Curtis LeMay, the mission of this unit is as follows:

> Members of the new Air Commando Group are trained to instruct allied aircrews in all phases of airborne operations, including low-level drop techniques for both personnel and cargo, close air support—in daylight or dark—for counterguerrilla forces, rapid deployment to areas of suspected or actual guerrilla activity, the use of flares for night-time detection of guerrilla movements and for reconnaissance, the cutting off of retreat routes by use of anti-personnel weapons, the staking out from the air of areas of suspected enemy activity, interdiction raids, destruction of supply points, and the use of psychological operations such as harassment and counter-information programs.
>
> Working alongside the Air Commando unit, the 1st Combat Applications Group is developing even more effective weapons for Air Commando use in seeking out and destroying guerrilla bands. This Group is assigned the development, testing and evaluation of new tactics and equipment for counterinsurgency use. The two Groups, working together, will develop weapon systems to be employed on particular missions and for special types of terrain.[8]

Like the Army Special Forces units, certain elements of the USAF's 1st Air Commando Group have already completed training and advisory missions in developing states (Mali and South Vietnam, for example). These special units, when combined with comparable American ground units and MAAG's, can play a vital role in providing counterinsurgency support assistance to foreign military forces.

Another specialized unit, the U.S. Army's Civil Affairs Mobile Training Team (CAMTT) can also provide significant support to these same forces in a different area of military activity nation-building. Drawn from the Civil Affairs Units of the United States Strategic Army Corps, these teams are assigned on a temporary basis to any MAAG that has requested their services. The composition of such a unit will vary from assignment to assignment and can run the gamut of civil affairs functional specialties, education, agriculture, finance, public administration, and public safety.

The pilot project for CAMTT actions was conducted in

Guatemala during 1961. In a sixty-day period this team conducted civic-action training programs in fourteen major Army commands, indoctrinating four hundred officers in the process, and prepared a comprehensive plan for such nation-building operations. Since the completion of this pilot project, several CAMTT units have been assembled and dispatched to Iran and various Southeast Asian nations.

There are still other specialized units with excellent potential for counterinsurgency-support establishments, particularly for operations directed against a Phase One Communist insurgency situation. Examples include the Preventive Medicine Companies of the United States Army, the Epidemiological Flights, Field Hospitals, and Meteorological Flights of the United States Air Force and other independent transportation, engineering, or communications units of the uniformed services.

A Proposal for a U.S. Counterinsurgency-Support Establishment

Now that we have surveyed the major resources available to the United States and the derived design criteria from the doctrinal prescriptions for counterinsurgency warfare—which were in part functions of the analyses of Communist insurgency in the developing nations—all that remains is to make recommendations for an American counterinsurgency structure. We realize that the creation of new agencies often brings about more problems than it solves; therefore, the recommendations below attempt to establish such a structure with a minimum of new creations and organizational dislocations.

The Washington Level—The necessity for a multidimensional approach (political, psychological, economic, and military) in United States counterinsurgency endeavors dictates that an interagency body continue to be employed at this level of American decision-making. The present Counterinsurgency

Task Force (a temporary body) should be transformed into a permanent interagency committee under the general direction of the Secretary of State. Its two principal and permanent members may be the deputy director of the Agency for International Development (AID) and the deputy Assistant Secretary of Defense for International Security Affairs (ISA). These two officers may rotate the chairmanship of this committee in accordance with the criteria presented below.

The other members of the committee should be organized into contingency-oriented Area Task Forces (ATF's) of a semipermanent nature, and these ATF's should have primary responsibility for specifically assigned regions of the underdeveloped world. Each task force should have approximately the following membership: one officer each from the appropriate area desk office of the AID, the USIA (United States Information Agency), the CIA (Central Intelligence Agency), and the ISA. There should be a representative from the Joint Chiefs of Staff, plus an additional Department of Defense ISA member who is specifically associated with the Office of the Director of Military Assistance. The chief of each such Area Task Force should be the senior member of the appropriate Area Affairs Office of the relevant Regional Bureau within the Department of State.

The chief of each ATF, because of his normal duties within the Department of State, will always have a current intelligence picture and an up-to-date national policy directive for his assigned area. Appreciative of his additional responsibilities as the head of a particular interagency counterinsurgency task force, he will tend to become more alert to indicators of insurgency and more demanding of intelligence support to his office. Potentially, therefore, each task force leader can provide the United States counterinsurgency establishment with a capability for rapid detection of insurgency in his area, thus providing the establishment with a capability for rapid, high-level policy response.

Each ATF can meet periodically to review relevant country plans and intelligence estimates related to insurgency probabilities in its assigned region. Once a Communist insurgency has been detected in its area of responsibility, the appropriate task force must closely monitor the situation. If the President of the United States receives a request for assistance from the government of the affected state, the ATF will play an important role through the Counterinsurgency Committee chairman and the Secretary of State in advising the Chief Executive as to the appropriate American response. If the President decides to aid this government, he may prescribe general policy to be implemented by the Secretary of State through the Counterinsurgency Committee. The relevant Area Task Force—as the main operative body of the committee—then will meet as frequently as necessary to provide staff assistance to this committee head for his general direction of American counterinsurgency support operations in the troubled area.

If support is directed against Phase One or Phase Two Communist insurgency, the chairman of the committee should be the deputy director of AID, and the vice-chairman should be the deputy Assistant Secretary of Defense for ISA. If an insurgency has developed into Phase Three—or, of course, Phase Four—the committee positions of these two officials should be reversed. The National Security Council (NSC) will determine the phase of insurgency development and recommend to the President (and hence the Secretary of State) the official who should chair the Counterinsurgency Committee for a particular contingency. This responsibility will be of a continuing nature, and the NSC will meet whenever the President, acting upon the advice of the Secretary of State or the Secretary of Defense, has determined that either progressive or retrogressive development has occurred which dictates a change in the subject chairmanship.

In the event that there are multiple and simultaneous insurgencies where two or more Area Task Forces are involved (that is, in support activities) and where the stages of insurgency vary from country to country, the President will similarly determine who will chair the Committee. However, in such situations the ranking Department of Defense member in each of the involved Area Task Forces should replace the State Department's senior representative as head of each unit when it is confronted with advanced-phase insurgency in its particular area. This rotating of key positions within the Counter-insurgency Committee and, in certain cases, within the ATF's themselves, should give the American counterinsurgency establishment a high-echelon directional flexibility that is essential for effective support endeavors against the cellular-development nature of Communist insurgency warfare.

Despite the impressive technical and executive talent which will always be resident within the Committee, once a particular insurgency has been detected and a response directed by the President, the Committee's active role in any prescribed support operations should be restricted to two essential functions. First, it should insure continual and expeditious administrative and logistics support to the establishment's field components. Second, it should formulate and promulgate policy guidance to be used by these component commanders. The very complexities and intimate nature of counterinsurgency warfare deny the Committee the quantity and quality of information needed on a continuing basis for it to get more directly involved in specific command and control processes. Consequently, this situation dictates the foregoing restrictions and the delegation of extensive command and control authority to the lower structural levels within the establishment.

The Unified Command Level—During American-supported operations against Phase One or Two insurgency, the relevant regional unified command will provide guidance on matters related to the Military Assistance Program. All other directives and policy guidance will go from Washington to the Country Team; the unified command will act only as an information addressee in these communications. Whereas the Counterinsurgency Committee will be headed by the Assistant Deputy Secretary of Defense for International Security Affairs (that is, during those periods when an American-supported incumbent regime is confronted with advanced-phase insurgency), the unified commander should be directly in the chain of command from Washington to the country level on all matters. However, as we mentioned before, the only level of military authority competent to exercise effective command over counterinsurgency-support operations is the "field force" at the country level itself. Hence the unified commander should do little more than modify the policy guidance from Washington by tailoring it to general considerations which from his vantage point reflect the current situation within his area of responsibility as a whole.

The unified command can make its greatest contributions to the American counterinsurgency establishment by quickly providing appropriate assistance to the field forces at the country level, such as the establishment and maintenance of substantial floating or fixed-supply depots. These depots, when combined with the Command's organic air transport, can expedite the delivery of essential military matériel, in any critical situation, to a country that has successfully solicited United States intervention in its internal war.

The unified command can also establish and maintain a Joint Counterinsurgency Force (JCF) directly subordinate to the commander-in-chief of each major regional unified command.

The core of each JCF should be an Army Special Forces group with supporting helicopter and light aircraft companies. An Air Commando group consisting of attack and transport squadrons should be part of this organization together with a small naval squadron of patrol craft and amphibious vehicles. Complementing these combat organizations should be an engineer construction battalion and detachments of civil affairs, medical, psychological warfare, intelligence, and communications personnel. In short, such a joint force should encompass virtually all the counterinsurgency capabilities possessed by the specialized military units previously described. The total personnel complement for this force will then be approximately two thousand men.

Each regional unified command JCF should operate its own counterinsurgency training center, which will teach foreign personnel all the techniques and tactics, ranging from patrol operations by hunter-killer units to military-civic action operations by teams of medical, engineering, and civil affairs personnel. Each force should have mobile training and support units (MTSU's) available for deployment to render all types of counterinsurgency-support to augment MAAG detachments in areas experiencing insurgency. These MTSU's can establish temporary training and assistance programs in those developing states desiring such aid but unwilling to enter into any long-term mutual-defense agreement with the United States.

The Army Special Forces training centers in Okinawa, Germany, and the Panama Canal Zone can become the embryo elements for the Joint Counterinsurgency Forces organizations in the relevant unified area commands. It is proposed that the commander-in-chief of STRICOM be authorized to establish an organic JCF that can be employed for counterinsurgency-support missions in sub-Saharan Africa and the Middle East. Since this Force will be tied to STRICOM's intercontinental air-mobility capability, it can also be a strategic reserve for its counterparts in the Pacific, European, and Latin American theaters.

A most important element of each JCF must be a theaterwise insurgency-intelligence collation and evaluation center. Such a center must receive all information relevant to insurgency in the developing nations within its unified command's general area of military jurisdiction. It will also provide intelligence support to deployed JCF elements.

The principal problems in the three regional unified commands mentioned earlier will involve personnel procurement.

Existing authorized force levels for the special warfare units of the Army and Air Force are too low to permit the creation of the three JCF's as proposed in this chapter. It is recommended, therefore, that these authorized strength restrictions be changed accordingly. The regional unified command can make still other vital contributions to the national counterinsurgency establishment. These contributions can be tied to the employment of its general purpose forces in such a manner as to deter the possible development of a particular insurgency from Phase Three to the final phase of conventional civil war. The deployment of American tactical air and ground forces to north Thailand, during the critical period in the development of the Pathet Lao insurgency in 1962, is an example of this operation. There may be cases in which the only possibility of saving an allied government from defeat caused by an unexpected and rapid development of an insurgency to Phase Four may lie in the employment by the United States—for her own security interests—of conventional forces in direct combat support of the indigenous counterinsurgents. Here the regional unified command or STRICOM can serve as the appropriate instrument for intervention.

In summary, the unified commands can and should play an important role in the counterinsurgency establishment proposed here by serving in key supporting roles and by providing deterrent power to inhibit the expansions of intermediate phase insurgency into civil war while at the same time not being in the direct line of military command between Washington and the field commander.

The Country Level—The American counterinsurgency establishment as outlined here will find itself most directly challenged in the country where insurgency operations are under way. Consequently, it is at this level that the establishment must be especially well organized and soundly operated. An important first step will consist of several preliminary activities to be undertaken by all American chiefs of diplomatic missions in developing states. Whether or not discernible symptoms of insurgency are already in evidence, each chief must see to it that the Country Team concept is formalized and solidified in his assigned country. To assist the ambassador in his expanded duties of supervision and coordination of the activities of this group, a special assistant should be appointed to serve as the secretary of the Country Team. He should preferably be a senior foreign service officer who has attended one of the War Colleges.

Under the direction of this special assistant, a comprehensive country plan should be drafted and subsequently revised on an annual or special circumstances basis. This plan must reflect the interrelationships among military, social economic, political, and psychological matters, and it must further reflect an appreciation of the contributions that the indigenous military, with appropriate American military training and advisory assistance, make toward the economic development of their nation. The plan itself should specify a coordination permitting maximum political exploitation of all American mission activities. Finally, the plan should provide for special operations and command relationships during insurgency contingency situations.

When the United States supports an incumbent regime threatened by Communist insurgency, the American ambassador in the troubled state must be given the maximum possible authority for the conduct of the counterinsurgency support operations. If the insurgency develops into Phase Three, this authority then may be transferred to the resident United States chief of MAAG or to the American military area commander if substantial United States military personnel are actually involved in these supporting endeavors. The recipient of this authority, however, must be made fully accountable for the effective application of American support resources. If his work is judged to be unsatisfactory by the Counterinsurgency Committee in Washington, he should be relieved and a successor appointed.

Two objections to these proposals on Country Team planning and operations become immediately apparent when one views the team within the over-all context of the conduct of United States foreign affairs. First, since there is often intense competition for resources among the various parent agencies at the Washington level and final decisions on the distribution of resources tend to be pushed upward to the President, resource allocations are often made on the general basis of "economic versus military aid." In other words, because the *specific* military and economic aid requirements of each particular foreign country (which will be reflected in the relevant country plan) are not normally considered at this high level, the dictates of each plan are generally meaningless. Second, the Country Team is an interdepartmental unit with no corresponding higher-echelon organization to which it is responsible or to which it can go for guidance and support.

The first objection, which obviously is well founded, can be overcome simply through Presidential authorization to the ambassador, the head of the team, to permit him a certain amount of flexibility in employing his assigned resources. For example, he should be permitted to use, within certain bounds, military aid resources for economic aid purposes and vice versa. The second objection can be met and overcome through the implementation at the Washington level of the organizational prescriptions for a Counterinsurgency Committee and Area Task Forces. These units will be interdepartmental in composition, and they will be compatible with their associated country teams in both organization and operation.

To complement this proposed Country Team command staff organization, it is essential to establish liaison with the appropriate indigenous counterpart organization, such as the planning or executive council of a National Emergency Committee. This will further insure that American counterinsurgency assistance is used to its maximum advantage in the defeat of the Communist insurgency. In moving from the general to the specific, but retaining the special focus on the military aspects of the counterinsurgency support establishment, it is recommended that the MAAG components of a Country Team in every developing state place greater emphasis on the number of combat engineer and civil affairs units to be incorporated into the tables of organization and equipment (TOE) of the indigenous forces. These units, of course, are to be used for accelerated and expanded civic-action programs, so MAAG unit composition itself should be changed accordingly. Further, it is recommended that these MAAG units expedite the creation and training of increased numbers of small local forces designed primarily for counterinsurgency operations and that they correspondingly decrease their emphasis on large forces trained to fight only conventional interstate wars. Finally, it is suggested that technical training programs for the indigenous forces be expanded and oriented as far as is militarily feasible to permit long-term integration with the demands for such expertise being generated by the developing national economy as a whole.

The Special Case of Intelligence—With the exception of the earlier proposal for an intelligence collection and evaluation center as part of the Joint Counterinsurgency Force in each of the regional unified commands, little attention has been given to this subject as it relates to the structure and operations of a United States counterinsurgency-support establishment. The reason for this relative neglect is that most of the pertinent organizational and operational information on intelligence activities is obviously classified. However, intelligence is so vital in counterinsurgency support operations that the subject must be discussed generally, regardless of this restriction and despite the fact that the recommendations offered here may already be in practice.

Timely response to requests for counterinsurgency support suggests that a regional (Unified Command JCF) and a national insurgency indications center be established for the entire underdeveloped world. Such agencies as the Central

Intelligence Agency, the Defense Intelligence Agency, and the State Department's Bureau of Intelligence and Research should undertake extensive interdisciplinary social science research projects that may lead to the discovery of even more pertinent indicators of insurgency in general and of Communist controlled insurgency in particular. The model of cellular development for Communist operations of this type suggests itself as a starting point.

The various collection agencies of the United States intelligence community must be apprised of the findings of these research activities so that the agencies can meaningfully direct their operations and effectively exploit their resources. The collection agencies should give priority to determining the political orientation of all insurgency potential organizations within the developing nations. It is most important that these agencies have the capability for deciding whether a government requesting counterinsurgency-support assistance from the United States is actually faced by Communist-controlled insurgency or by a genuine popular uprising that threatens the privileges and position of a traditional oligarchy. In many cases the insurgency will most likely reflect both these dimensions, but it is important for Washington to have an informed estimate of the degree to which Communists are promoting instability or supporting insurgent elements.

The American intelligence community must be able to alert the United States counterinsurgency-support establishment to impending insurgencies. It should have detailed information to assist the President in determining whether invited intervention will be in the best interests of the United States and the affected developing state. Finally, it should furnish the intelligence which will assist the establishment in tailoring its support operations to solve the specific problem at hand.

In concluding this chapter, one is tempted to think that, as the United States develops a doctrine and forces to deter

Communist states from initiating strategic and limited war against the Western Alliance, similarly the creation of an American counterinsurgency establishment will deter the Soviet Union and Communist China from launching Communist insurgency wars in the developing states. This, however, will not necessarily be the case. The organizational structure by itself will have little deterrence value. Its capabilities, when combined with enlightened reform and development programs of a threatened incumbent regime in a developing state, should significantly increase the effectiveness of this establishment in its deterrence role.

9

Summary and Conclusions

This book has had two purposes: first, to analyze the nature of Communist insurgency warfare in the developing areas; second, to propose an effective counter to this threat for both the developing nations and the United States.

The underlying argument has been that the probability of Communist insurgency warfare in a given developing state is related to three principal factors. The first is conflicting ideology, which has both an external and an internal dimension. It is external in that it is a reflection of the intensity of the international Cold War, and it is internal in that it reflects the intensity of the political-ideological conflict between indigenous Communist forces and the incumbent regime. The degree to which local Communist insurgents are dependent upon an international center of Communism for support will determine which dimension predominates.

The second factor, an external dimension, is simply the nuclear deterrence stalemate between East and West. The more stable the strategic situation, the more probable will be the initiation of Communist insurgencies sponsored and heavily supported by Moscow or Peiping.

Internal instability, itself a complex composite of many subfactors, is the third contributing factor. The greater the sociopolitical instability within an emerging state, the more probable will be the use by local Communists of these forces for their own ends. Other factors of course contribute to this warfare, but these three are the most important. By viewing Communist insurgency warfare in this general perspective, the West can understand it better and counter it more successfully.

The *mystique* that appears to surround this phenomenon and the body of Communist theory related to it is definitely unjustified. This type of warfare in general and guerrilla operations in particular are not new designs of international Communism to meet the requirements for offensive actions under the restrictive limitations of mutual terror in the nuclear space age. They are, rather, adaptations of traditional principles of irregular warfare—adopted because of pragmatic necessity and wedded by shotgun to Marxist-Leninist dogma.

Lenin himself provides the genesis for the Communist version of insurgency warfare by proclaiming that the modes of revolutionary conflict must conform directly to their respective historical eras. He contends that successful Communist revolutions will most likely occur through protracted conflict, during which the powers of an incumbent regime will systematically be eroded away. Then Mao Tse-tung eclectically draws tactics and techniques from past historical episodes of irregular warfare and supplies the philosophical core—find strengths in one's own weaknesses and weaknesses in the enemy's strengths. From this he constructs a body of viable strategic and tactical prescriptions for insurgency in the mid-twentieth century. Although modified by Vo Nguyen Giap (international considerations) and Ernesto Guevara (the urban dimension), the central principle remains that this form of conflict rests on the ideological mobilization of the masses.

Through the careful synthesis of pertinent Communist theory with relevant Communist practice, it is possible to construct a model of this phenomenon. Communist insurgency warfare, roughly speaking, expands as cells develop. The four phases of growth are infiltration-subversion, small armed band operation, insurrection, and civil war. The following capsule condensations summarize the essence of this cellular thesis.

Phase One—The critical element in the initiatory phase is the acquisition of insurgency leadership. This leadership generally is derived from disenchanted but highly nationalistic intellectuals. After receiving Communist indoctrination, this element seeks to discredit the existing government and social system. It then endeavors to crystallize and channel the amorphous forces of mass discontent, and, finally, compels the forces of change to follow a predetermined Communist pattern. In doing so, it poses an immediate psychopolitical threat to the incumbent regime. At the same time, it secretly prepares for guerrilla warfare should this prove necessary in Phase Two.

Phase Two—Crystallization of discontent among the populace and the organization of the actively discontented that occurred in the first phase are translated into insurgent military capability in the second phase. Thus rural villages, and some urban centers, have formed within them small armed bands and complementary logistics and intelligence support units. These guerrilla forces, without the benefit of meaningful unitary operational control, launch against the government armed raids aimed at alienating the people from the existing regime. Finally, through these military and psychological operations, the guerrillas expand the insurgency-affected areas and prepare the physical battleground for the succeeding stage.

Phase Three—This phase is characterized by the establishment of a large, secure base area (or several areas) in which the insurgent organization actually replaces the control of the incumbent regime with its own administrative apparatus. It is marked by an almost feverish pitch of activity to stockpile supplies obtained from internal sources and greatly expanded (relatively speaking) contributions from external sources. Recruitment is stepped up dramatically; regular force units are created, or guerrilla forces are regularized, and these forces begin their training preparatory to their entry into the next phase as conventional units. Finally, the military activities consist of large-scale and well-coordinated guerrilla operations in which sophisticated tactics are used and military considerations seem to predominate over political considerations in the selection of targets. In short, Phase Three is essentially an expansive guerrilla-type preparation for the final victory phase, civil war.

Phase Four—Total replacement of the incumbent regime by the insurgent forces is the objective of this fourth and final phase. Its most noticeable characteristic is the transformation of the military conflict from guerrilla warfare to conventional limited war.

This four-phase, cellular development thesis can be viewed as a model for the growth of a typical Communist insurgency in an underdeveloped state: the sequential processes of crystallization, organization, and militarization can be considered as the energizing elements that give the insurgency expanded and directed development from phase to phase.

There are two arguments against this thesis. Do the leader-states of international Communism initiate such insurgency wars, or do they merely attach their claims in a very astute manner to a general socioeconomic revolution that is not the prerogative of any particular ideology? The answer is they do both. Even if their capability is restricted to the latter, however, proper utilization of the cellular model may well indicate when such a Communist claim is being made and the impact it has upon the insurgency movement as it pertains to domestic objectives and international orientation. The second argument concerns the unusual characteristics of those insurgencies already recorded in the pages of history and the diverse characteristics of the underdeveloped states, the future targets. These complex characteristics cannot be denied, but they should not exclude analysis.

Some important common denominators emerge from any

study in depth of recorded Communist insurgency wars. Significantly, many important common denominators can be found in a careful study of the problems and aspirations of underdeveloped states regardless of their differences in geographical location or culture.

In constructing this conceptual scheme, the focus has been upon these common denominators. Thus this scheme provides a framework of insurgency which, if it is to be meaningfully applied to a particular state, must be modified and expanded according to the peculiarities of that state.

Since the end of World War II, counterinsurgency warfare by the West has usually been haphazard, experimental, and "play-it-by-ear" in nature. The reason for this, it seems, can be found in a lack of proper understanding of Communist insurgency by the West. The model described here—which places this phenomenon in proper national (or local) and international perspective—can appreciably assist the West in understanding this threat. Hopefully, better operations will follow.

An incumbent regime in an insurgency-troubled nation, for example, must view the threat to its existence as a part of the composite four-phase strategy of Communist insurgency. By appreciating the cellular nature of this threat, the regime will act swiftly. Their actions will be based on the contention that armed bands (Phase Two insurgency) are merely self-seeking bandits. The costs of mounting operations against such bands operating in remote areas will seem too high in relation to the other pressing requirements for government resources; yet if an insurgency is permitted to grow and develop, the costs for later counteroperations will be dramatically higher, and the impact upon national sociopolitical and economic stability will be much more grave. Realizing the highly political nature of this conflict, the incumbent regime will not be satisfied with military measures alone. It will institute reforms and economic development to alleviate the popular grievances upon which the insurgency feeds.

The government will best order and orient its response to

Phase Two or Phase Three insurgency by directing its actions toward the achievement of three principal objectives: expansion of control over the populace; weakening and exposure of the insurgent-guerrilla forces; engagement and defeat of the guerrilla units in military combat. These objectives are interrelated and will have to be pursued simultaneously at both strategic and tactical levels of conflict.

Subsequent to consolidating its position in terms of both land held under control and allegiance pledged by the populace, the government must systematically expand its control over those persons who seem apathetic or are actually sympathetic to the insurgent cause. Through quick-impact and easily discernible social reforms and economic development (as applicable to a given situation) and appropriate psychological-action campaigns, it can effectively and progressively attain this goal. The regime must involve as many of the people as possible. As political allegiances increase, these people can be converted into a dedicated manpower pool that can be called upon to fill the ranks of paramilitary units and local police forces. These forces can then relieve professional military personnel from general security duties, thus permitting them to expand the regime's direct military control over outlying guerrilla-infested regions.

In attaining the second objective, which is directly tied to the first, programs of fortified villages and resettlement operations can be carried out. Thus more people will come under the government's physical control. If these actions are complemented by reform and development programs sponsored and subsidized by the regime, this control can become psychopolitical in nature. Once this is accomplished, the traditional sources of guerrilla strength—intelligence, food, recruits—will be denied to these insurgent forces. Consequently, they will be considerably weakened in terms of their military and psychopolitical power.

Another important action—denying external support to

the insurgents—can be accomplished by proper control over the land, air, and sea approaches to guerrilla base areas. Finally, an indirect method of weakening the enemy will be the strengthening of the incumbent regime through military and economic development assistance from an industrially advanced ally. This outside aid, however, must not resemble a "colonial situation," which of course is excellent grist for the insurgent propaganda mill.

The guerrilla forces, weakened and continually losing strength, will be forced to revert to the tactics of earlier phases —justified by Mao's concept of revolutionary flow—or to enlarge prematurely their operational forces by consolidating existing resources rather than adding new components of strength. If they revert to earlier tactics, they are faced with the realistic probability that continued government-sponsored reforms and economic development programs will deny them the conditions and resources necessary for later expansion and progression. If they consolidate resources, they are prematurely moving their operations to a more advanced phase. Such operations, before the popular base has been adequately prepared, will ease the government's task of seeking out, isolating, and destroying the insurgent-guerrilla field units. In order to obtain popular support for their expanded actions, the insurgents may be forced to forget Mao Tse-tung's dictum of treating the people as brothers. They may quite conceivably resort to terror, which, while it may bring transitory successes, may also bring long-term liabilities. Instead of being fish in an ocean of friendly people, the insurgents will become fish out of water, vulnerable and destined for an early and violent death.

In operations designed to achieve the third goal—engagement and defeat of the guerrilla forces—small-scale rather than large-scale surface operations (encirclement and sweep) stand the better chance for success. The reasons for this can be found in the topographical nature of the areas where insurgency potential is highest. Also, the armies in the affected areas usually will be able to carry out only the small-scale actions in anything resembling an effective manner.

Static-defense positions which do not support continuing offensive patrol actions by the counterinsurgents seem to be continuing liabilities to the regime. This is somewhat related to the dictum that commanders of field units committed to patrol actions be given maximum authority to exploit exposed guerrilla targets. Each encounter that is forced upon the insurgent units and is not a result of their own calculations stands an excellent chance of government victory.

The employment of airpower in support of operations to defeat the insurgent field forces can indeed be decisive and instrumental in the achievement of the first and second goals of counterinsurgency operations. Surface forces should be decentralized to be most effective; air forces, however, should be centralized. This will enable the emerging state to use its limited airpower to maximum advantage.

Once an intermediate phase insurgency has been defeated through the highly coordinated activities of civil and military forces, the regime must consolidate its victory by eliminating or weakening the destabilizing forces which induce local Communists to start Phase One insurgency operations. In short, after the defeat of the guerrilla field forces, the government must assume that a Phase One insurgency threat still exists. It cannot afford to be lulled back into complacency simply because order has been restored and the populace seems content with its new-found security. The initial grievances of the populace must still be answered effectively.

This Phase One threat will not be much different from the situation in emerging states which have not experienced advanced phase insurgency but are faced with the threat in its incipient stage. In both cases the local armed forces present the incumbent regime with a resource for change, reform, and nation-building—a resource that can significantly supplement the attempts of civil agencies to attain these stabilizing objectives. Unfortunately, this resource has been employed only in a very modest way within the developing world.

The armed forces, with their organization, communications, facilities, discipline, and geographic dispersion, can bring meaningful cohesion to a new nation-state. The harnessing of their technological and administrative expertise for constructive endeavors can significantly enhance the government's capabilities for meeting the expectations of the populace. These constructive endeavors can range from small-scale construction projects, technical-agricultural assistance, and medical-sanitation programs by outlying garrisons to major infrastructure projects by engineer units of the local army—assisted perhaps by foreign military advisers. The educational programs include the acculturative processes to which the recruits are subjected, technical training for military personnel, and utilization of officers and noncommissioned officers as teachers in remote areas which do not attract civil educators. Finally, military personnel can often be employed in public administration posts that cannot be filled because of a lack of trained civil servants.

These constructive military endeavors can, of course, be carried out without the incumbent regime's substantially increasing its normal expenditures to support the armed forces. Such noncombat military activities, however, can bring serious problems as well as rewards. For example, the use of troop labor may have an unfavorable impact upon the working community within a state. Extensive military operations in infrastructure projects and transportation activities may stifle the development of viable civil engineering and commercial transport enterprises. Continued reliance upon the military for public administration functions can conceivably retard, if not destroy, the development of a conscientious civil-servant corps responsive and responsible in a politically meaningful manner to the civil government. Finally, excessive and long-term utilization of troops in noncombat endeavors may seriously impair the fighting quality of the nation's military establishment.

Nevertheless, if the military forces are properly controlled and directed by civil authorities cognizant of some of the pitfalls of these civil-military activities, then an incumbent regime can use the military in a most effective and constructive manner to defeat a Phase One insurgency or even to preclude it from ever occurring.

It is imperative that United States counterinsurgency operations remain essentially indirect and supportive in character. An over zealous attempt by pragmatic Americans to support directly and overwhelmingly a troubled incumbent government may well bring about a defeat rather than a victory for the Free World.

The United States must create and structure a counterinsurgency-support establishment that can detect Communist insurgency in its early stages of development and can quickly deliver the assistance authorized by the President. Because of the cellular nature of the development of Communist insurgency, early action can bring about victory with a minimum expenditure of indigenous and externally supplied resources. The limited nature of external support will tend to enhance the palatability of this assistance as viewed by an affected government concerned with its people's fears of neocolonialism. The consequent limited involvement of the United States will make this assistance more palatable to the prestige-conscious and economy-conscious American people.

This American establishment should consist of a Counterinsurgency Committee composed of the Secretary of State, the Deputy Assistant Secretary of Defense for International Security Affairs, the Deputy Director of the Agency for International Development, and several area-oriented task forces of interagency composition. The next level should be the regional unified command. This agency should contain an interservice Joint Counterinsurgency Force with training and combat operations capabilities. This Command should be responsible for maintaining on-the-spot reservoirs of counterinsurgency support—both matériel and personnel—to provide additional de-

terrent power, thus inhibiting the expansion of specific
Communist insurgencies to the final phase of civil war.

The lowest level of this support establishment is the country itself. Here the United States Country Team should be
organized as a command and staff entity with the American
ambassador as its chief. In advanced insurgency, the senior
United States military officer in the area should assume this
command position. In either case the head of the Country
Team should be made responsible for American support to the
beleaguered state and accordingly should be held accountable
for all activities of the team during counterinsurgency operations.

In conclusion, it is appropriate to state again that the
threat of Communist insurgency warfare will exist and con-
front the United States, and the West in general, throughout
the decade of the 1960's and perhaps even into the 1970's. It
will occur in some developing states where popular expectations are not being sufficiently satisfied by the incumbent
regime. It will also occur in some developing states when reform and development programs—for example, those prescribed by the Alliance for Progress in Latin America—begin
to take hold and thus start to foreclose Communist insurgency
opportunities. Such warfare may also occur whenever either
the Soviet Union or Communist China find themselves unable
to pursue a national foreign policy objective because of an effective Western deterrence or, more simply, when they think they
can get away with it. For example, Communist China's lack
of a long-range logistics capability may compel her to use this
means to achieve certain high-priority objectives in Latin
America or Africa. The Soviet Union's attempts to disrupt the
European Economic Community may well take the form of
sponsored insurgency warfare in those African states which
provide the Common Market with the bulk of its natural
resources.

It is certainly true that no two Communist insurgencies

will be exactly alike. The same can be said, however, of many medical and social problems which have in fact been solved by the application of therapy that focuses on common denominators of similar problems while making allowances for discernible differences on a case-by-case basis. The prescriptions we present, therefore, must not be viewed as schoolbook solutions to be slavishly followed. Neither should they be viewed as solutions to be disregarded immediately because the abstraction upon which they are based does not at first glance seem to conform to the reality of a particular situation.

Our hope is that by utilizing the material in this book solutions to some Communist insurgency problems will be found —that an ordering, a systematization, and a proper orientation for counterinsurgency operations will be developed. That the United States should lead in these endeavors is dictated by the fact that it is the leader of the Free World. That it must succeed in these endeavors is dictated by the fact that the values it wishes to preserve at home and to promote abroad are directly challenged by the threat of Communist insurgency warfare in the developing areas of the world.

NOTES

Notes

1. INTRODUCTION

1. "Guerrilla Warfare in Theory and Policy," *Modern Guerrilla Warfare*, Franklin Mark Osanka, editor (New York: The Free Press of Glencoe, 1962), p. 1.
2. Cuba does not truly fit into this mold; the Cuban Communist Party did not actively support the Castro revolution until it was well on its way to success. Nevertheless, "Che" Guevara and Raoul Castro, two Communists, were in the vanguard of this Cuban revolution, and they facilitated the voluntary Communist takeover of the *Fidelismo* movement in postrevolutionary Cuba. See Dickey Chapelle, "How Castro Won," *Marine Corps Gazette*, 44:36–44, February 1960, and United States Department of State, *Cuba:* Publication 7171 (Washington: Government Printing Office, April 1961).

2. FACTORS CONTRIBUTING TO COMMUNIST INSURGENCY WARFARE: A COLD WAR PERSPECTIVE

1. United States Congress, Senate, *A Summary and Interpretive Analysis of Khrushchev's Speech of 6 January 1961* prepared by the Legislative Reference Service, Library of Congress. Senate Document No. 14, 87th Congress, 1st Session (Washington: Government Printing Office, 1961), p. 18.
2. *Ibid.*, p. 25.
3. *Ibid.*
4. Cited in U. Alexis Johnson, "Cold War World," *Airman*, 6:35, May 1962.
5. *New York Times*, February 18, 1962.
6. U.S. Congress, House, *Department of Defense Appropriations for 1963*, Hearings Before Subcommittee of the Committee on Appropriations, Part 2 (Washington: Government Printing Office, 1962), p. 7.
7. "Internal War, The New Communist Tactics," *Military Review*, 42:12, April 1962.

8. Translated extracts reprinted in the *Manchester Guardian Weekly*, January 10, 1963.
9. Joseph B. Gittler, "Social Adjustment to Technological Innovation," *New Era in Non-Western World*, W. S. Hunsberger, editor (Ithaca, N.Y.: Cornell University Press, 1957), p. 4.
10. See Edward Shils, "The Intellectuals in the Political Development of the New States," *World Politics*, 12:132, April 1960.
11. This study is specifically concerned with Communist insurgency; therefore no attempt will be made to propose a universal standard of evaluation which will permit analysts to distinguish non-Communist (*e.g.*, FLN) insurgency from Communist insurgency. However, it is suggested that the model of Communist insurgency presented in Chapter 4 will have utility in such interdisciplinary endeavors.

3. THE EVOLUTION OF COMMUNIST THEORY
ON INSURGENCY WARFARE:
AN HISTORICAL PERSPECTIVE

1. Joseph P. Kutger, "Irregular Warfare in Transition," *Military Affairs*, 24:113–123, Fall 1960.
2. Peter Paret and John W. Shy, *Guerrillas in the 1960's* (New York: Frederick A. Praeger, 1962), pp. 12–13.
3. G. O. Miksche, *Secret Forces* (London: Faber & Faber, 1959), p. 25.
4. James D. Atkinson, "The Communist Revolution in Warfare," *U.S. Naval Institute Proceedings*, 79:286–287, March 1953.
5. Translated by Regina Eldor, in *Modern Guerrilla Warfare*, Franklin Mark Osanka, editor (New York: The Free Press of Glencoe, 1962), pp. 65–79. (This translation originally appeared in the Summer edition of *Orbis*, 1958.)
6. *Ibid*, p. 67.
7. *Ibid.*, p. 78.
8. *Ibid.*, p. 68.
9. James D. Atkinson, *The Edge of War* (Chicago: Henry Regnery, 1960), p. 64.
10. E. L. Katzenbach, Jr., and Gene Z. Hanrahan, "The Revolutionary Strategy of Mao Tse-tung," *Political Science Quarterly*, 70:323, September 1955.
11. R. L. Garthoff, "Unconventional Warfare in Communist Strategy," *Foreign Affairs*, 40:569, July 1962.
12. Samuel B. Griffith, "Introduction," *Mao Tse-tung on Guerrilla Warfare* (New York: Frederick A. Praeger, 1961), p. 25.
13. *Ibid*.
14. Mao Tse-tung, "On Protracted War," *Selected Works*, Volume II (New York: International Publishers, 1954), p. 192.
15. Katzenbach and Hanrahan, *op. cit.*, p. 326.
16. S. B. Griffith (trans.), *Mao Tse-tung on Guerrilla Warfare* (New York: Frederick A. Praeger, 1961), p. 96.
17. *Ibid*.
18. *Ibid.*, p. 98.
19. *Ibid.*, pp. 101–102.
20. *Ibid.*, p. 104.

21. *Ibid.*, pp. 105–107.
22. *Ibid.*, p. 107.
23. Cited in Soixante, "Defeat in the East," *Journal, Royal United Services Institution*, 106:362, August 1961.
24. *Mao Tse-tung on Guerrilla Warfare, op. cit.*, p. 111.
25. Cited in Soixante, *op. cit.*, p. 363.
26. *Mao Tse-tung on Guerrilla Warfare, op. cit.*, p. 114.
27. Samuel B. Griffith, editor and translator, "Mao's Primer on Guerrilla War," *Marine Corps Gazette*, 46:44, January 1962.
28. *Selected Works*, Volume II, *op. cit.*, p. 204.
29. Katzenbach and Hanrahan, *op. cit.*, p. 327.
30. "On the Rectification of Incorrect Ideas in the Party," *Selected Works*, Volume I, *op. cit.*, p. 106.
31. Cited by Edward G. Lansdale, "Southeast Asia." Lecture at the U.S. Army War College, Carlisle Barracks, Pennsylvania, December 3, 1958.
32. *Mao Tse-tung on Guerrilla Warfare, op. cit.*, p. 93.
33. *Ibid.*, p. 85.
34. *Ibid.*, p. 86.
35. Katzenbach and Hanrahan, *op. cit.*, p. 332.
36. *Mao Tse-tung on Guerrilla Warfare, op. cit.*, p. 65.
37. These excerpts from Giap's *People's War, People's Army* were extracted from the condensed version of this book that appeared under the title "Inside the Vietminh," *The Guerrilla and How to Fight Him*, Lt. Colonel T. N. Greene, editor (New York: Frederick A. Praeger, 1962), pp. 147–161.
38. Garthoff, *op. cit.*, p. 10.
39. G. K. Tanham, *Communist Revolutionary Warfare: The Vietmink in Indochina* (New York: Frederick A. Praeger, 1961), pp. 14–21.
40. *La Guerra de Guerrillas* (translated by the editors of the journal *Army*). Excerpts reproduced in *Readings on Guerrilla Warfare* (Fort Bragg, North Carolina: U.S. Army Special Warfare School, 1960), p. J–2.
41. *Ibid.*, pp. J–20, 21.
42. *Ibid.*, pp. J–1, 2.
43. *Che Guevara on Guerrilla Warfare* (New York: Frederick A. Praeger, 1961), p. 67.
44. Harries-Clichy Peterson, "Introduction," *Che Guevara on Guerrilla Warfare, ibid.*, p. xiii.
45. *Ibid.*, p. 66.
46. *La Guerra de Guerrillas, op. cit.*, pp. J–13, 14.
47. *Ibid.*, pp. J–14, 15.
48. *Ibid.*, p. 3.
49. *Ibid.*, p. 75.
50. Cited in Harries-Clichy Peterson, *op. cit.*, p. xii.
51. Garthoff, *op. cit.*, p. 7.

4. A SYNTHESIS OF COMMUNIST THEORY AND PRACTICE:
A THEORY OF CELLULAR DEVELOPMENT

1. *America's Strategy in World Politics* (New York: Harcourt, Brace & World, 1942).

2. Morris Watnick, "The Appeal of Communism to the Underdeveloped Peoples," in *Progress of Underdeveloped Areas*, Bert F. Hoselitz, editor (Chicago: University of Chicago Press, 1962), pp. 152–174.
3. Cited in *Ibid.*, p. 170.
4. Klaus Knorr, "Unconventional Warfare: Strategy and Tactics in Internal Political Strife," *Annals of the American Academy of Political and Social Science*, 341:59, May 1962.
5. Government of the Federation of Malaya, *The Communist Threat to the Federation of Malaya* (Kuala Lumpur: Government Press, 1959), pp. 2–8.
6. Ralph L. Muros, "Communist Terrorism in Malaya," *U.S. Naval Institute Proceedings*, 87:54, October 1961.
7. For an excellent and detailed discussion of this general form of Phase Two organization as it applies to South Vietnam, see United States Government, *A Threat to the Peace*, U.S. Department of State Publication 7308 (Washingon: Government Printing Office, 1961), pp. 7–20.
8. For a documented inventory of the tremendous amount of military hardware that has come over the Ho Chi Minh trail from North Vietnam through eastern Laos and into South Vietnam, see United States Government, *A Threat to the Peace, op. cit.*, pp. 32–33.
9. For an excellent analysis of the motivational factors that drove young Chinese to join the Communist insurgency movement in Malaya, see Lucian W. Pye, *Guerrilla Communism in Malaya* (Princeton: Princeton University Press, 1956).
10. Virgil Ney, "Guerrilla War and Modern Strategy," *Orbis*, 2:10, Spring 1958.
11. Dickey Chapelle, "How Castro Won," *Marine Corps Gazette*, 44:40, February 1960.
12. In the non-Communist EOKA operations in Cyprus during the late 1950's and in the Zionist activities in Palestine in the late 1940's, terrorism alone led to a victory for the insurgent forces.
13. William H. Hessler, "Guerrilla Warfare Is Different," *U.S. Naval Institute Proceedings*, 88:38, April 1962.
14. J. K. Zawodny, "Guerrillas and Sabotage: Organization, Operations, Motivation, Escalation," *Annals of the American Academy of Political and Social Science*, 341:10, May 1962.

5. THE COMBAT ROLE OF THE MILITARY: SURFACE OPERATIONS

1. These computations were completed by Colonel George M. Jones. They appear in the September 1959 issue of the *Special Warfare Center Newsletter* of Fort Bragg, North Carolina.
2. Claude Witze, "USAF Polishes Its New COIN," *Air Force and Space Digest*, 45:50, June 1962.
3. Bernard Fall, "Revolutionary Warfare in Southeast Asia," *Readings in Guerrilla Warfare* (Fort Bragg, North Carolina: U.S. Army Special Warfare School, 1960), p. 156.
4. George B. Jordan, "Objectives and Methods of Communist Guerrilla Warfare," *Military Review*, 39:53, January 1960.
5. William H. Hessler, "Guerrilla Warfare Is Different," *U.S. Naval*

Institute Proceedings, 88:35, April 1962. This ratio reflects an incorporation of Militia and Home Guards into the counterinsurgent force totals.

6. United States Government, *A Threat to the Peace*. Department of State Publication 7308 (Washington: Government Printing Office, 1961), p. 6.

7. Edwin F. Black, "Problems of Counterinsurgency," *U.S. Naval Institute Proceedings*, 88:35, October 1962.

8. Tomas C. Tirona, "The Philippine Anti-Communist Campaign: A Study of Democracy in Action," *Air University Quarterly Review*, 7:42–55, Summer 1954.

9. Peter Paret and John W. Shy, *Guerrillas in the 1960's* (New York: Frederick A. Praeger, 1962), p. 49.

10. Gene Z. Hanrahan, "Japanese Operations Against Guerrilla Forces," *Technical Memorandum ORO-T-268* (Baltimore: Johns Hopkins University, 1954), pp. 14–16.

11. E. G. Lansdale, *Civic Action Activities of the Military*, Southeast Asia Subcommittee of the Draper Committee (Washington: Government Printing Office, 1959) and Government of the Republic of the Philippines, *EDCOR Plan* (Quezon City: Department of National Defense, n. d.).

12. For an excellent evaluation of this particular program, especially as it pertains to its long-term consequences, see Hamzah-Sendut, "Rasah—A Resettlement Village in Malaya," *Asian Survey*, 1:21–26, November 1961.

13. Occasionally there may be a deviation from this rather normal pattern of reluctance to leave native soil. For example, as reported in the *Times of Viet Nam*, August 5, 1962, over 96,000 Vietnamese highlanders (Montagnards), who traditionally have been reluctant to face modern civilization, voluntarily requested resettlement in the safer lowlands.

14. For descriptions of supplemental food control programs in Malaya during the Emergency, see Ralph L. Muros, "Communist Terrorism in Malaya," *U.S. Naval Institute Proceedings*, 87:51–57, October 1961, and Government of Canada, "The Emergency in Malaya," *External Affairs*, 13:87–92, March 1961.

15. For an account of the Republic of Vietnam's operations in this regard, see United States Government, *A Threat to the Peace*, *op. cit.*, pp. 23–37.

16. For an English translation of this manual, see C. Aubrey Dixon and Otto Heilbrunn, *Communist Guerrilla Warfare* (New York: Frederick A. Praeger, 1954), Appendix, Article 56.

17. Thoung Htaik, "Encirclement Methods in Counterguerrilla Warfare," *Military Review*, 41:90–95, June 1961.

6. AIR OPERATIONS AND GENERAL ORGANIZATION

1. For a more detailed discussion of these criteria, see General Gough's article, "Airpower and Counterinsurgency," *Airman*, 6:2–7, August 1962.

2. *Ibid.*, p. 6.

3. *Air Power and Russian Partisan Warfare*, U.S.A.F. Historical Studies

No. 177 (Maxwell Air Force Base, Alabama: Research Studies Institute, Air University, 1962), p. 20 and Human Resources Research Institute, Air Research and Development Command, "The Role of Airpower in Partisan Warfare," *U.S.A.F. Counterinsurgency Course: Selected Reading* (Maxwell Air Force Base, Alabama: Air University, 1962), pp. v–2–11 to v–2–13.

4. Ione Leigh, *In the Shadows of the Mau Mau* (London: W. H. Allen Co., Ltd., 1954), p. 197.
5. Human Resources Research Institute, ARDC, "The Role of Airpower in Partisan Warfare," *op. cit.*, p. v–2–13.
6. K. R. C. Slater, "Air Operations in Malaya," *Journal of the Royal United Service Institution*, 102:379, August 1957.
7. R. J. Blackburn, "Aircraft Versus Mau Mau," *Flight*, 66:710, November 12, 1954.
8. *Times of Viet Nam*, July 13 and 21, 1962.
9. Slater, *op. cit.*, p. 380.
10. *Ibid.*, p. 377.
11. Boyd T. Bashore, "Vertical Counter-Attack by Counter-Insurgents," *Army*, 12:23–27, April 1962.
12. *Ibid.*
13. "Report from Viet Nam," *Army*, 13:22, September 1962.

7. THE NONCOMBAT ROLE OF THE MILITARY

1. Cf. Jason L. Finkle, "Civil-Military Relations in Viet Nam." Address to the National Conference of the American Society for Public Administration, Detroit, Michigan, April 12, 1962.
2. For example, see Brigadier General Donald G. Shingler's study which appears as "Annex D" of *Composite Report of the President's Committee to Study the United States Military Assistance Program* (Washington: Government Printing Office, 1959); Lucian W. Pye, *Armies in the Process of Political Modernization*, Monograph (Cambridge, Massachusetts: Center for International Studies, Massachusetts Institute of Technology, 1959).
3. Robert H. Slover, "Civic Action in the Era of the Cold War." Lecture at the Military Assistance Institute, Arlington Towers, Arlington, Virginia, March 14, 1961.
4. Edward G. Lansdale, "Civic Action." Lecture at the Counter-Guerrilla School, Special Warfare Center, Fort Bragg, North Carolina, February 24, 1961.
5. Lucian W. Pye, *op. cit.*, p. 9.
6. *Ibid.*, p. 10.
7. *Ibid.*, p. 11.
8. United States Department of the Army, Office of the Chief of Civil Affairs, *Report of Civic Action Team for Guatemala* (Washington: Department of the Army, 1961).
9. Robert H. Slover, *loc. cit.*
10. *Composite Report of the President's Committee to Study the United States Military Assistance Program*, Vol. II, *op. cit.*, p. 120.
11. Lucian W. Pye, *op. cit.*, p. 14.
12. *Ibid.*, p. 15.
13. *Ibid.*

14. *New York Times*, November 8, 1959.
15. See John Badgley, "Burma's Military Government," *Asian Survey*, 2:31, August 1962, and D. P. Singhal, "The New Constitution of Pakistan," *Asian Survey*, 2:19–23, August 1962.
16. B. T. Bashore, "Dual Strategy for Limited War," *Military Review*, 40:62, May 1960, and E. G. Lansdale, "The Free Citizen in Uniform." Address at the U.S. Army Civil Affairs School, Fort Gordon, Georgia, November 1, 1960.
17. Frank Tannenbaum, "On Political Stability," *Political Science Quarterly*, 75:169, June 1960.

8. AN AMERICAN COUNTERINSURGENCY ESTABLISHMENT

1. Cited in Boyd T. Bashore, "Dual Strategy for Limited War," *Military Review*, 40:60, May 1960.
2. Edward Katzenbach, Jr., and Gene Hanrahan, "The Revolutionary Strategy of Mao Tse-tung," *Political Science Quarterly*, 70:324, September 1955.
3. "Guerrilla Warfare in the Underdeveloped Areas," *The Department of State Bulletin*, 45:237, August 7, 1961.
4. S. P. Huntington, *Instability at the Non-Strategic Level of Conflict*, Research Memorandum No. 2 (Washington: Institute for Defense Analysis, 1961), p. 37.
5. United States Congress, Senate, Committee on Foreign Relations, *Additional Materials on Administration of the Department of State*, 87th Congress, 2nd Session (Washington: Government Printing Office, 1962), pp. 2–3.
6. Cited in Paul D. Adams, "Strike Command," *Military Review*, 42:6, May 1962.
7. United States Congress, House, Committee on Appropriations, *Department of Defense Appropriations for 1963*, Hearings, 87th Congress (Washington: Government Printing Office, 1962), p. 344.
8. "Announcement by the Chief of Staff, USAF, Los Angeles, 27 April 1963," Press Release by the Office of Information Services, Headquarters, United States Air Force, April 27, 1962.

BIBLIOGRAPHY

Bibliography

Primary Sources

DOCUMENTS

Ball, George W. *Viet-Nam: Free World Challenge in Southeast Asia.* Department of State Publication 7388. Washington: Government Printing Office, 1962.

Bayo, Giroud Alberto. *One Hundred and Fifty Questions Asked of a Guerrilla Fighter.* New York: U.S. Joint Publications Research Service, 1959.

Civil Affairs in the Cold War. Special Study No. 151. Operations Research Office. Bethesda, Maryland: Johns Hopkins University, 1961.

Civil Affairs in Future Armed Conflicts. Operations Research Office. Bethesda, Maryland: Johns Hopkins University, 1960.

Clausewitz, Carl von. "Volksbewaffnung," *On War.* Book IV. Trans. O. S. Matthis Jolles. Washington, D.C.: Combat Forces Press, 1950.

"Commissariat General for Cooperation and Agricultural Credit," *The Times of Viet-Nam Magazine*, 4:13–16, July 22, 1962. Government Document, Republic of Viet-Nam. Newspaper reprint.

Condit, D. M. *Case Study in Guerrilla War: Greece During World War II.* Special Warfare Research Division, Special Operations Research Office. Washington: The American University, 1961.

Drum, Karl D. *Air Power and Russian Partisan Warfare*. USAF
Historical Studies No. 177. Maxwell Air Force Base, Alabama:
Research Studies Institute, Air University, 1962.

Giap, Vo Nguyen. *People's War, People's Army*. Hanoi: Foreign
Languages Publishing House, 1961.

Gilpatric, Roswell L. "Relation of Southeast Asia to the Free
World," *Air Force Information Policy Letter, Supplement for
Commanders*, 107:13–17, June 15, 1962.

Government of Canada, Department of External Affairs. "The
Emergency in Malaya," *External Affairs*, 13:87–92, March
1961.

Government of the Federation of Malaya. *The Communist Threat
to the Federation of Malaya*. Legislative Council Paper No. 23
of 1959. Kuala Lumpur: Government Press, 1959.

Government (Royal) of Laos. *Lao Royal Armed Forces Training
Manual for Civic Action Teams*. Trans. Major Victor L. Oddi,
U.S. Army. Vientiane, Laos: U.S. Military Assistance Advis-
ory Group, 1960.

Government of the Republic of the Philippines, Department of
National Defense. *The EDCOR Plan*. Camp Murphy, Quezon
City, Republic of the Philippines: Office of the Chief, Eco-
nomic Development Corps, 1950.

Government of the Republic of Viet-Nam. *Major Policy Speeches
by President Ngo Dinh Diem*. Saigon: Press Office of the
Presidency, 1957.

———. *News From Viet-Nam*. A publication of the Press and
Information Office, Embassy of the Republic of Viet-Nam,
10:2–21, September 1961, and 8:4–16, April 1962.

———. *The Problem of Reunification of Viet-Nam*. Saigon: Ministry of Information, 1958.

———. *Seven Years of the Ngo Ninh Diem Administration, 1954–
1961*. Saigon: Ministry of Information, 1961.

———. *Viet-Nam Review*. A publication of the Press and Information Office, Embassy of the Republic of Viet-Nam, 1:1–16,
August 9, 1962, and 1:1–8, June 6, 1962.

———. *Violations of the Geneva Agreements by the Viet-Minh
Communists from July 1959 to June 1960*. Saigon: Kimlai An
Quan, 1960.

Guevara, Che. *On Guerrilla Warfare*. Trans. U.S. Department of
the Army and the Marine Corps Association. New York: Frederick A. Praeger, 1961.

Hanrahan, Gene Z. "Japanese Operations Against Guerrilla Forces," *Technical Memorandum ORO–T–268*. Operations Research Office. Baltimore: Johns Hopkins University, March 16, 1954.

Khrushchev, Nikita S. "For New Victories of the World Communist Movement," *Kommunist*, January 1961. Translated version published under the title *Khrushchev Report on Moscow Conference of Representatives of Communist and Workers Parties*. Washington: Government Printing Office, 1961.

Lansdale, Edward G. *Civic Activities of the Military, Southeast Asia.* Memorandum to the Anderson-Southeast Asia Subcommittee of the Draper Committee. Washington: Government Printing Office, March 13, 1959.

Le Matériel Aéronautique, 1961. Vol. I. Paris: Union Syndicate des Industries Aeronautiques, 1961.

LeMay, Curtis E. "Airpower in Guerrilla Warfare," *Air Force Information Policy Letter, Supplement for Commanders,* 16:1, April 15, 1962.

———. "South Viet-Nam and Counterinsurgency," *Air Force Information Policy Letter, Supplement for Commanders,* 107:1–9, June 15, 1962.

Lenin, V. I. "Partisanskaya Voina," Vol. X of *Sochineniya.* Trans. Regina Eldor. Reprinted in *Modern Guerrilla Warfare,* edited by Franklin Mark Osanka. New York: The Free Press of Glencoe, 1962.

Mao Tse-tung. *Guerrilla Warfare (Yu Chi Chan).* Trans. Brigadier General Samuel B. Griffith. New York: Frederick A. Praeger, 1961.

———. *Selected Works.* Vols. I and II. New York: International Publishers, 1954.

Modelski, George. *The International Relations of Internal War.* Research Monograph No. 11. Center of International Studies. Princeton: Princeton University Press, 1961.

Natsinas, Alexander. *Guerrilla Warfare: The Organization and Employment of Irregulars.* Greece: U.S. Army Service Group Detachment, Intelligence Section, 1950.

Nhu, Ngo Dinh. "Progress in Liberty and Justice, Through Liberty and Justice, and Despite the Communist Aggression," *The Times of Viet-Nam Magazine,* 4:4–6, August 5, 1962. Publication of First Lady Madame Ngo Dinh Nhu's address to the first graduating class of the Women's Paramilitary Force.

O'Meara, Andrew P. "Internal Order in Latin America," *Air Force*

Policy Letter, Supplement for Commanders, 105:38–40, May 16, 1962. Statement of the Commander-in-Chief, Caribbean Command, before the House Foreign Affairs Committee, March 22, 1962.

Outline of a Civil Assistance Program. Vientiane, Laos: U.S. Military Assistance Advisory Group, 1961.

Pye, Lucian W. "Armies in the Process of Political Modernization." Unpublished Monograph. Center for International Studies, Massachusetts Institute of Technology, Cambridge, Massachusetts, 1959.

Rostow, W. W. "Guerrilla Warfare in the Underdeveloped Areas," *The Department of State Bulletin*, 45:233–238, August 7, 1961.

Rusk, Dean. "The Major Obstacle to Peace," *Air Force Information Policy Letter, Supplement for Commanders*, 107:10–11, June 15, 1962.

————. "Civil Affairs in the Area of Cold War," *Congressional Record*, 107:1–9, June 27, 1961.

Slover, Robert H. "Civic Action in the Era of the Cold War." Lecture at the Military Assistance Institute, Arlington Towers, Arlington, Virginia, March 14, 1961.

Southeast Asia Treaty Organization. *Community Development.* Bangkok, Thailand: SEATO Headquarters, 1960.

United Nations. *Community Development and Economic Development*, Part I. Bangkok, Thailand: UN Publication, 1960.

United States Army Special Warfare School. *Readings in Counterguerrilla Operations.* Fort Bragg, North Carolina: Special Warfare Center, 1961.

————. *Readings in Guerrilla Warfare.* Fort Bragg, North Carolina: Special Warfare Center, 1960.

United States Congress, House. *Foreign Aid.* 86th Congress, 1st Session, H.R. 116. Washington: Government Printing Office, June, 1959.

United States Congress, House, Committee on Appropriations. *Department of Defense Appropriations for 1963.* Hearings Before Subcommittee, Part 2. Washington: Government Printing Office, 1962.

United States Congress, House, Committee on Foreign Affairs. *The International Development and Security Act, Part II.* 87th Congress, 1st Session, H.R. 732. Washington: Government Printing Office, 1961.

————. *Castro Communist Subversion in the Western Hemisphere.*

88th Congress, 1st Session, H.R. 55. Washington: Government Printing Office, 1963.

United States Congress, Library of Congress, Legislative Reference Service. *US Foreign Aid: Its Purposes, Scope, Administration, and Related Information.* 86th Congress, 1st Session, H.R. 116. Washington: Government Printing Office, 1959.

United States Congress, Senate. *Public Law 87–195.* Foreign Assistance Act of 1961. 87th Congress, S. 1983, September 4, 1961. Washington: Government Printing Office, 1961.

United States Congress, Senate, Committee on Foreign Relations. *Additional Materials on Administration of the Department of State.* 87th Congress, 2nd Session. Washington: Government Printing Office, July 31, 1962.

———. "Economic, Social and Political Change in the Underdeveloped Countries and Its Implications for United States Policy," *United States Foreign Policy,* pp. 1165–1268. 86th Congress, 2nd Session. Washington: Government Printing Office, 1960.

———. "Ideology and Foreign Affairs," *United States Foreign Policy.* 86th Congress, 2nd Session. Washington: Government Printing Office, 1960.

———. *Peace Corps Act Amendments.* Hearings, 87th Congress, 2nd Session. Washington: Government Printing Office, 1962.

———. *Punta Del Este Conference, January, 1962.* Report, 87th Congress, 2nd Session. Washington: Government Printing Office, 1962.

———. "Some Observations on the Operation of the Alliance for Progress: The First Six Months," *United States-Latin American Relations.* 87th Congress, 2nd Session. Washington: Government Printing Office, 1962.

———. *Study Mission in the Caribbean and Northern South America, November, 1959.* 86th Congress, 1st Session. Washington: Government Printing Office, 1960.

———. *Viet Nam and Southeast Asia.* 88th Congress, 1st Session. Washington: Government Printing Office, 1963.

United States Congress, Senate, Committee on Government Operations. *Administration of National Security.* 88th Congress, 1st Session. Washington: Government Printing Office, 1963.

United States Congress, Senate, Committee on the Judiciary. *Analysis of the Khrushchev Speech of January 6, 1961.* Hearings, 87th Congress, 2nd Session. Washington: Government Printing Office, 1961.

United States Congress, Senate, Special Committee to Study the Foreign Aid Program. "Foreign Assistance Activities of the Communist Bloc and Their Implications for the United States," *Foreign Aid Program,* pp. 619–766. 85th Congress, 1st Session. Washington: Government Printing Office, 1957.

—————. "The Military Assistance Program of the United States: Two Studies and a Report," *Foreign Aid Program,* pp. 881–1056. 85th Congress, 1st Session. Washington: Government Printing Office, 1957.

United States Department of the Air Force. "Announcement by Chief of Staff, USAF, Los Angeles, 27 April 1962," News Release OI–62–88. Langley Air Force Base, Virginia: Tactical Air Command, Office of Information, April 28, 1962.

—————. *Military Assistance Program: Information and Guidance.* Washington: Government Printing Office, 1962.

—————. *USAF Airborne Operations, World War II and Korean War.* Washington: USAF Historical Division Liaison Office, 1962.

United States Department of the Air Force, Air Research and Development Command. *The Role of Airpower in Partisan Warfare.* Maxwell Air Force Base, Alabama: Human Resources Research Institute, December 1954.

United States Department of the Air Force, Air University. *Communist Attempts at Discrediting Americans.* Maxwell Air Force Base, Alabama: Research Studies Institute, 1962.

—————. *Strategic Briefs.* Maxwell Air Force Base, Alabama: Research Studies Institute, 1961.

—————. *USAF Counterinsurgency Course Text: Selected Readings.* Maxwell Air Force Base, Alabama: Air University, 1962.

United States Department of the Air Force, Tactical Air Command. *Joint Air-Ground Operations.* TACM 55–3. Langley Air Force Base, Virginia: Headquarters Tactical Air Command, 1957.

United States Department of the Army. *Field Service Regulations, Doctrinal Guidance.* Field Manual 100–1. Washington: Government Printing Office, 1959.

—————. *Field Service Regulations, Operations.* Field Manual 100–5. Chapters 10, 11, and 12. Washington: Government Printing Office, 1962.

—————. *Format for a Psychological Warfare Country Plan.* Washington: Government Printing Office, 1954.

—————. *German Anti-Guerrilla Operations in the Balkans (1941–1944).* Pamphlet 2–243. Washington: U.S. Department of the Army, 1954.

213   Bibliography

———. *Guerrilla and Counter-Guerrilla Warfare in Greece, 1941–1945.* Manuscript, Office of the Chief of Military History. Washington: Government Printing Office, 1961.

———. *Guerrilla Warfare and Special Forces Operations.* Field Manual 31–21. Washington: Government Printing Office, 1958.

———. *Operations Against Irregular Forces.* Field Manual 31–15. Washington: Government Printing Office, 1961.

———. *The Soviet Partisan Movement, 1941–1944.* Pamphlet 20–244. Washington: Government Printing Office, 1956.

United States Department of the Army, Office of the Chief of Civil Affairs. *Report of Civic Action Team for Guatemala.* Washington: U.S. Department of the Army, 1961.

United States Department of State. *Cuba.* U.S. Department of State Publication 7171. Washington: Government Printing Office, April 1961.

———. *A Threat to the Peace.* U.S. Department of State Publication 7308. Washington: Government Printing Office, 1961.

United States Government. *Executive Order 10973 (Administration of Foreign Assistance and Related Functions).* Washington: Government Printing Office, 1961.

———. *The Lesson of Cuba.* Department of State Publication 7185. Washington: Government Printing Office, 1961.

———. *Special Message on Defense Budget to the Congress of the United States, 28 March 1961.* Washington: Government Printing Office, 1961.

United States Government, President's Task Force on Foreign Economic Assistance. *Act for International Development: A Summary Presentation.* Washington: Government Printing Office, 1961.

Wolf, Charles, Jr. *Some Connections Between Economic and Military Assistance Programs in Underdeveloped Areas,* P–2389. Santa Monica, California: The RAND Corporation, 1961.

GENERAL

Adams, Paul D. "Strike Command," *Military Review,* 42:2–10, May 1962.

Bethouart, Hilaire. "Combat Helicopters in Algeria," *The Guerrilla —And How to Fight Him,* Lt. Colonel T. N. Greene, editor. New York: Frederick A. Praeger, 1962.

Boynton, Willard H. "For Better Health in Viet Nam," *The Times of Viet-Nam Magazine,* 4:18–19, August 12, 1962.

Gough, Jamie. "Airpower and Counterinsurgency," *Airman*, 6:2–7, August 1962.

Harriman, Averell W. "What We Are Doing in Southeast Asia," *The New York Times Magazine*, May 27, 1962.

Htaik, Thoung. "Encirclement Methods in Counterguerrilla Warfare," *Military Review*, June 1961. Reprinted in *Special Warfare: U.S. Army*. Washington: Government Printing Office, 1962.

Johnson, U. Alexis. "Cold War World," *Airman*, 6:33–36, May 1962.

Khan, Ayub Mohammed. "Pakistan Perspective," *Foreign Affairs*, 38:541–556, July 1960.

Lawrence, T. E. "The Arab Revolt of 1916–18," *Encyclopaedia Britannica*, X, 950–950D.

LeMay, Curtis E. "Counter Insurgency and the Challenge Imposed," *Airman*, 6:2–9, July 1962.

Slater, K. R. C. "Air Operations in Malaya," *Journal of the Royal United Service Institution* (United Kingdom), 102:378–387, August 1957.

Yarborough, W. P. "Young Moderns Are Impetus Behind Army's Special Forces," *Army*, 14:1–4, March 1962.

UNPUBLISHED MATERIALS

Bohannan, C. T. R. "Unconventional Operations." Seminar presentation on anti-HUK campaign, Fort Bragg, North Carolina, June 15, 1961.

Decker, George H. "The Military Situation Confronting the Western Hemisphere." Remarks at Inter-American Army Conference, Panama Canal Zone, July 10, 1961.

Howze, Hamilton H. "Counterinsurgency Warfare." Presentation to the Imperial Defense College, London, May 18, 1962.

Jones, Roger W. "Civic Action." Address to the graduating class of the U.S. Army Civil Affairs School, Fort Gordon, Georgia, March 2, 1962.

Justiniano, Medardo T. "Combat Intelligence in the Campaign Against the Communist HUKS." Seminar presentation, Fort Bragg, North Carolina, June 15, 1961.

Lansdale, Edward G. "Civic Action." Lecture, Counter-Guerrilla School, Special Warfare Center, Fort Bragg, North Carolina, February 24, 1961.

————. "The Free Citizen in Uniform." Address at the U.S. Army Civil Affairs School, Fort Gordon, Georgia, November 1, 1960.

215

Bibliography

———. "The Insurgent Battlefield." Address at the U.S. Air Force Academy, Colorado, May 25, 1962.

———. "Introductory Comments on the Campaign." Seminar presentation on the HUK campaign, Fort Bragg, North Carolina, June 15, 1961.

———. "Southeast Asia." Lecture at the U.S. Army War College, Carlisle Barracks, Pennsylvania, December 3, 1958.

Lapus, Ismael D. "The Communist Huk Enemy." Seminar presentation on the HUK campaign, Fort Bragg, North Carolina, June 15, 1961.

McGhee, George C. "Strategy of American Foreign Policy." Address before the San Francisco Area World Trade Association, World Trade Club, San Francisco, California, March 27, 1962.

Mead, A. D. "The Changing Role of Civil Affairs." Address to the Military Government Association National Convention, St. Paul, Minnesota, May 20, 1961.

Valeriano, Napoleon D. "Military Operations Against the HUKS." Seminar presentation, Fort Bragg, North Carolina, June 15, 1961.

Secondary Sources

BOOKS

Amery, Julian. *Sons of the Eagle, a Study in Guerrilla War.* London: The Macmillan Company, 1948.

Atkinson, James D. *The Edge of War.* Chicago: Henry Regnery, 1960.

Crozier, Brian. *The Rebels: A Study of Post War Insurrections.* London: Chatto and Windus, 1960.

Dixon, C. Aubrey, and Otto Heilbrunn. *Communist Guerrilla Warfare.* New York: Frederick A. Praeger, 1954.

Fall, Bernard B. *Street Without Joy: Indochina at War, 1946–54.* Harrisburg, Pennsylvania: Stackpole Company, 1961.

Heilbrunn, Otto. *Partisan Warfare.* New York: Frederick A. Praeger, 1962.

Higgins, Benjamin. *Indonesia's Economic Stabilization and Development.* New York: Institute of Pacific Relations, 1957.

Johnson, John J., ed. *The Role of the Military in Underdeveloped Countries.* Princeton: Princeton University Press, 1962.

Lawrence, Thomas E. *Seven Pillars of Wisdom, A Triumph.* Garden City, N.Y.: Garden City Publishing Company, 1938.

Lieuwen, Edwin. *Arms and Politics in Latin America*. London: Oxford University Press, 1960.

Miksche, F. O. *Secret Forces*. London: Faber and Faber, 1959.

Ney, Virgil. *Notes on Guerrilla War: Principles and Practices*. Washington, D.C.: Command Publications, 1961.

1962, the Year of the Strategic Hamlets. Saigon: Times of Viet-Nam Press, 1962.

Osanka, Franklin Mark, ed. *Modern Guerrilla Warfare*. New York: The Free Press of Glencoe, 1962.

Paret, Peter, and John W. Shy. *Guerrillas in the 1960's*. New York: Frederick A. Praeger, 1962.

Pye, Lucian W. *Guerrilla Communism in Malaya*. Princeton: Princeton University Press, 1956.

Smedley, Agnes. *The Great Road: The Life and Times of Chu Teh*. New York: Monthly Review Press, 1956.

Spykman, N. J. *America's Strategy in World Politics*. New York: Harcourt, Brace and World, 1942.

Staley, Eugene. *The Future of Underdeveloped Countries: Political Implications of Economic Development*. New York: Frederick A. Praeger, for the Council on Foreign Relations, 1961.

Tanham, George K. *Communist Revolutionary Warfare: The Viet-minh in Indochina*. New York: Frederick A. Praeger, 1961.

Taylor, Maxwell D. *The Uncertain Trumpet*. New York: Harper and Row, 1960.

Ward, Barbara. *The Rich Nations and the Poor Nations*. New York: W. W. Norton, 1962.

PERIODICALS AND ARTICLES IN COLLECTIONS

Arnold, Theodore. "The Technique of the Revolutionary War," *Bulletin of the Institute for the Study of the USSR*, 7:3–12, November 1960.

Atkinson, James D. "The Communist Revolution in Warfare," *U.S. Naval Institute Proceedings*, 79:285–291, March 1953.

Badgley, John. "Burma's Military Government: A Political Analysis," *Asian Survey*, 2:24–31, August 1962.

Bashore, Boyd T. "Dual Strategy for Limited War," *Military Review*, 4:46–62, May 1960.

——. "Vertical Counter-Attack by Counter Insurgents," *Army*, 12:23–30, April 1962.

Beebe, John E., Jr. "Beating the Guerrilla," *Military Review*, 35:3–18, December 1955.

Bellah, James. "Encirclement by Air," *Infantry Journal*, 54:9–13, June 1944.

Bellinger, John B., Jr. "Civilian Role in Antiguerrilla Warfare," *Military Review*, 41:91–94, September 1961.

Benda, Harry J. "Revolution and Nationalism in the Non-Western World," *New Era in the Non-Western World*, Warren S. Hunsberger, editor. Ithaca, N.Y.: Cornell University Press, 1957.

Bjelajac, Slavko N. "Soviet Activities in Underdeveloped Areas," *Military Review*, 61:57–61, February 1961.

———. "Soviet Unconventional Warfare Capabilities," *Military Review*, 39:30–37, November 1959.

———. "Unconventional Warfare: American and Soviet Approaches," *Annals of the American Academy of Political and Social Science*, 341:74–81, May 1962.

Black, Edwin F. "Problems of Counterinsurgency," *U.S. Naval Institute Proceedings*, 88:22–41, October 1962.

Blackburn, Robert J. "Aircraft Versus Mau Mau," *Flight*, 66:707–710, November 12, 1954.

Blendheim, Sven. "The Strategy of Underground Warfare," *Militaer Orientering*, December 15, 1950. English translation appears in *Military Review*, 37:77–79, June 1951.

Braestrup, Peter. "Partisan Tactics—Algerian Style," *Army*, 11:33–44, August 1960.

Brooke, F. H. "Infantry and Air Power in Malaya," *Australian Army Journal*, 67:15–17, December 1954.

Burr, Robert N., ed. "Latin American Nationalistic Revolution," *Annals of the American Academy of Political and Social Science*, 334, March 1961.

"Cas Concrets de Guerre Revolutionnaire," *Revue Militaire d'Information*, 281:15–36, February–March 1957.

"The Changing Role of the Military in Colombia," *Journal of Inter-American Studies*, 3:351–358, July 1961.

Chapelle, Dickey. "How Castro Won," *Marine Corps Gazette*, 44:36–44, February 1960.

Clutterbuck, R. L. "The Change in the Pattern of Land Warfare," *Army Quarterly* (United Kingdom), 81:161–181, January 1961.

Courtenay, W. "Army Aviation in Malaya," *Canadian Aviation*, 29:31–32, May 1956.

Crockett, Anthony. "Action in Malaya," *Marine Corps Gazette*, 39:309–319, January 1955.

Davis, Paul C. "Political Warfare and the Global Struggle," *Readings in Guerrilla Warfare*. Fort Bragg, North Carolina: U.S. Army Special Warfare School, 1960.

Delaney, Robert F. "A Case for a Doctrine of Unconventional Warfare," *U.S. Naval Institute Proceedings*, 87:66–71, September 1961.

D'Encausse, Carrere H. "Iranian Tudeh," *Revue Militaire d'Information*, 281:48–61, February–March 1957.

Dougherty, James E. "The Guerrilla War in Malaya," *U.S. Naval Institute Proceedings*, 84:40–41, September 1958.

Drancourt, Michel. "France's Army in Algeria: Its Morale, Its Social Mission," *Realities*, pp. 1–4, April 1959.

Dziuba, I. S., *et al.* "Partisan Warfare," *Military Review*, 38:107–109, January 1959.

Fall, Bernard. "Revolutionary Warfare in Southeast Asia," *Readings in Guerrilla Warfare*. Fort Bragg, North Carolina: U.S. Army Special Warfare School, 1960.

Falls, Cyril. "Greek Army and the Guerrillas," *Military Review*, 27:73–76, March 1948.

Fishel, Wesley R. "Political Realities in Vietnam," *Asian Survey*, 1:15–24, April 1961.

Fricker, John. "High Level Helicopter Operations in Kenya," *The Aeroplane*, 88:296–297, March 11, 1955.

Fuller, Francis F. "Mao Tse-tung: Military Thinker," *Military Affairs*, 22:139–145, Fall 1958.

Garthoff, Raymond L. "Unconventional Warfare in Communist Strategy," *Foreign Affairs*, 40:566–575, July 1962.

Gittler, Joseph B. "Social Adjustment to Technical Innovation," *New Era in Non-Western World*, Warren S. Hunsberger, editor. Ithaca, N.Y.: Cornell University Press, 1956.

Halpern, Joel M. "Observations on the Social Structure of the Lao Elite," *Asian Survey*, 1:25–32, July 1961.

Hamzah, Sendut. "Rasah—A Resettlement Village in Malaya," *Asian Survey*, 1:21–26, November 1961.

Hanrahan, Gene Z. "The Chinese Red Army and Guerrilla Warfare," *Combat Forces Journal*, 1:10–13, February 1951.

Hendry, James B. "Economic Development Under Conditions of Guerrilla Warfare: The Case of Viet Nam," *Asian Survey*, 11:1–12, June 1962.

Hessler, William H. "Guerrilla Warfare Is Different," *U.S. Naval Institute Proceedings*, 88:35–48, April 1962.

Hilsman, Roger. "Internal War, The New Communist Tactic," *Military Review*, 42:11–22, April 1962.

Jacobs, Walter Darnell. "Mao Tse-tung As a Guerrilla: A Second Look," *Military Review*, 37:26–30, February 1958.

Jonas, Anne M., and George K. Tanham. "Laos: A Phase in Cyclic Regional Revolution," *Orbis*, 5:64–73, Spring 1961.

Katzenbach, Edward L., Jr. "Time, Space and Will: The Politico-Military Views of Mao Tse-tung," in *The Guerrilla—And How to Fight Him*, Lt. Colonel T. N. Greene, editor. New York: Frederick A. Praeger, 1962.

————, and Gene Z. Hanrahan. "The Revolutionary Strategy of Mao Tse-tung," *Political Science Quarterly*, 70:321–340, September 1955.

Kelly, George A. "Revolutionary Warfare and Psychological Action," in *Modern Guerrilla Warfare*, Franklin Mark Osanka, editor. New York: The Free Press of Glencoe, 1962.

Kleinman, Forrest K. "Report from Viet-Nam," *Army*, 13:21–36, September 1962.

————. "This is Strike Command," *Army*, 12:14–16, April 1962.

Kling, Merle. "Cuba: A Case Study of a Successful Attempt to Seize Political Power by the Application of Unconventional Warfare," *Annals of the American Academy of Political and Social Science*, 341:42–52, May 1962.

Knorr, Klaus. "Unconventional Warfare: Strategy and Tactics in Internal Political Strife," *Annals of the American Academy of Political and Social Science*, 341:53–64, May 1962.

Kraemer, Fritz G. A. "U.S. Propaganda: What It Can and Can't Be," *Stanford Research Institute Journal*, Fourth Quarter, 1959.

Kutger, Joseph P. "Irregular Warfare in Transition," *Military Affairs*, 24:113–123, Fall 1960.

Leaske, T. "The Problems of Cold War Operations," *The Army Quarterly* (United Kingdom), July 1957.

Lindsay, Franklin A. "Unconventional Warfare," *Foreign Affairs*, 40:264–274, January 1962.

Linebarger, Paul M. A. "Indochina: The Bleeding War," *Combat Forces Journal*, 1:32–36, March 1951.

von Luttichau, Charles. "Some Observations on Guerrilla Warfare in Russia During World War II," *Readings in Guerrilla Warfare*. Fort Bragg, North Carolina: U.S. Army Special Warfare School, 1960.

McKinley, Webb. "Cyprus: How the Greek Underground Kept the British Army Unhappy," *USAF Counterinsurgency Course: Selected Reading*. Maxwell Air Force Base, Alabama: Air University, 1962.

Marshall, Charles Burton. "Unconventional Warfare as a Concern of American Foreign Policy," *Annals of the American Academy of Political and Social Science*, 341:93–101, May 1962.

Mellema, R. L. "The Basic Democracies System in Pakistan," *Asian Survey*, 1:10–15, August 1961.

Muros, Ralph L. "Communist Terrorism in Malaya," *U.S. Naval Institute Proceedings*, 87:51–57, October 1961.

Neilan, Edward. "Village Defense," *The Times of Viet-Nam Magazine*, 4:9, July 22, 1962.

"New Airborne Eyes for the Foot Soldier," *The Times of Viet-Nam Magazine*, 4:18–19, July 29, 1962.

Ney, Virgil. "Guerrilla War and Modern Strategy," *Orbis*, 2:66–82, Spring 1958.

Papagos, Alexander. "Guerrilla Warfare," *Foreign Affairs*, 30:215–230, January 1952.

Pye, Lucian W. "The Non-Western Political Process," *Journal of Politics*, 20:38–52, August 1958.

Rhyne, Russell. "Patterns of Subversion by Violence," *Annals of the American Academy of Political and Social Science*, 341:65–73, May 1962.

Robinson, R. E. R. "Reflections of a Company Commander in Malaya," *The Army Quarterly* (United Kingdom), 61:81–87, October 1960.

Rostow, W. W. "Countering Guerrilla Warfare," *New Leader*, 44:12–14, July 31–August 7, 1961.

Schwarz, Walter. "The Cold War and the African States," *Commentary*, 33:505–512, June 1962.

Seymour, W. N. "Terrorism in Malaya," *The Army Quarterly* (United Kingdom), 58:109–113, April 1949.

Sherwani, Latif Ahmed. "The Constitutional Experiment," *Asian Survey*, 2:9–14, August 1962.

Shils, Edward. "The Intellectuals in the Political Development of the New States," *World Politics*, 12:329–368, April 1960.

Singhal, D. P. "The New Constitution of Pakistan," *Asian Survey*, 2:15–23, August 1962.

Soixante. "Defeat in the East," *Journal of the Royal United Services Institute* (United Kingdom), 106:355–371, August 1961.

Souyris, Andre. "An Effective Counterguerrilla Procedure," *Revue de Defense Nationale,* June 1956. English translation in *Military Review,* 36:86–90, March 1957.

Spark, Michael. "Guerrillas, Small Wars, and Marines," *Marine Corps Gazette,* 46:50–54, January 1962.

Stewart, H. Douglas. "How to Fight Guerrillas," *U.S. Naval Institute Proceedings,* 88:22–37, July 1962.

Tannenbaum, Frank. "On Political Stability," *Political Science Quarterly,* 75:161–180, June 1960.

Taylor, Maxwell D. "Our Changing Military Policy," *Army,* 12:54–56, March 1962.

Teichert, Pedro C. M. "Latin America and the Socio-economic Impact of the Cuban Revolution," *Journal of Inter-American Studies,* 2:105–120, January 1962.

Thorpe, William J. "HUK Hunting in the Philippines 1946–1953," *Air Power Historian,* 9:95–100, April 1962.

Thuc, Vu Quoc. "National Planning in Vietnam," *Asian Survey,* 1:3–9, September 1961.

Tirona, Thomas C. "The Philippine Anti-Communist Campaign: A Study of Democracy in Action," *Air University Quarterly Review,* 7:42–55, Summer 1954.

Wainhouse, Edward. "Guerrilla Warfare in Greece, 1946–1949: A Case Study," *Military Review,* 37:17–25, June 1957.

Watnick, Morris. "The Appeal of Communism to the Underdeveloped Peoples," *The Progress of Underdeveloped Areas,* Bert F. Hoselitz, editor. Chicago: University of Chicago Press, 1952.

Whitaker, Arthur P. "Protracted Conflict in Latin America," *Orbis,* 6:301–310, Summer 1962.

Wilkins, Frederick, "Guerrilla Warfare," *U.S. Naval Institute Proceedings,* 80:311–318, March 1954.

Williams, Robin M., Jr. "Are Americans and Their Cultural Values Adaptable to the Concept and Techniques of Unconventional Warfare?" *Annals of the American Academy of Political and Social Science,* 341:82–92, May 1962.

Witze, Claude. "USAF Polishes Its New Coin," *Air Force and Space Digest,* 45:46–52, June 1962.

Wolf, Charles, Jr. "Public Policy and Economic Development in the Philippines," *Asian Survey,* 1:35–38, December 1961.

Ximenes. "La Guerre Révolutionnaire et ses Données Fondamentales," *Revue Militaire d'Information,* 281:9–29, February–March 1957.

Zawodny, J. K. "Guerrillas and Sabotage: Organization, Operations, Motivation, Escalation," *Annals of the American Academy of Political and Social Science*, 341:8–18, May 1962.

UNPUBLISHED MATERIALS

Bagnulo, Aldo H. "The Country Team." Unpublished thesis, U.S. Army War College, Carlisle Barracks, Pennsylvania, 1960.

Beard, Willard F. "The Employment of Air Power in Anti-Guerrilla Warfare." Unpublished thesis, Air University, Maxwell Air Force Base, Alabama, 1962.

Boak, David G. "Guerrillas in Latin America." Unpublished thesis, Air University, Maxwell Air Force Base, Alabama, 1961.

Cross, James Eliot. "The Challenge of Unconventional Warfare." Address to a meeting of the Council on Religion and International Affairs, Washington, D.C., October 31, 1961.

De Long, Robert E. "Guerrilla Warfare and Tactical Air: An Appraisal." Unpublished thesis, Air University, Maxwell Air Force Base, Alabama, 1962.

Finkle, Jason L. "Civil-Military Relations in Vietnam." Address to the National Conference of the American Society for Public Administration, Detroit, Michigan, April 12, 1962.

Itschner, E. C. "The Army Engineers' Contribution to American Defense and Advancement." Address at the Annual Dinner of Washington Newcomers, Mayflower Hotel, Washington, D.C., April 3, 1959.

Kennedy, Kenneth W. "Civic Action as a Cold War Weapon." Unpublished thesis, U.S. Army War College, Carlisle Barracks, Pennsylvania, 1962.

Lewis, W. A. "Economic Development and Social Peace." Lecture at the University of Chile, April 6, 1962.

Millikan, Max F. "New and Old Criteria for Aid." Address before the Academy of Political Science, November 28, 1961.

Nguyen, Huy Anh. "A New Outlook on the Use of the Helicopter in Southeast Asia Guerrilla Warfare." Unpublished study, Air University, Maxwell Air Force Base, Alabama, 1962.

Rabenold, Ellwood M. "The Country Team as an Instrument for Political Influence." Unpublished thesis, Air University, Maxwell Air Force Base, Alabama, 1961.

Smedlie, Joseph A. "Economic Derivatives of Military Aid in Underdeveloped Countries." Unpublished thesis, U.S. Army War College, Carlisle Barracks, Pennsylvania, 1960.

Stanley, Richard E. "A Concept of Anti-Guerrilla Operations in Indo-China." Unpublished study, Command and Staff College, Air University, Maxwell Air Force Base, Alabama, 1961.

NEWSPAPERS

Bigart, Homer. "America's Involvement Grows with Drastic Measures Designed to Thwart Further Communist Expansion," *The New York Times*, April 1, 1962.
————. "U.S. Now Acquiesces in President Diem's Demands But Many Americans Remain Critical," *The New York Times*, June 3, 1962.
"A Growing Navy," *The Times of Viet-Nam Magazine*, 4:6–8, July 22, 1962.
The New York Times, November 8, 1959; January 5, 1962; January 7, 1962; September 11, 1962.
Oganesoff, Igor. "On the Edge of Battle," *The Wall Street Journal*, March 6, 1962.
"A Review of the Major Industrial Projects," *The Times of Viet-Nam Magazine*, 4:19, August 5, 1962.
Rose, Jerry A. "The Peasant is the Key to Vietnam," *The New York Times Magazine*, pp. 23 *passim*, April 8, 1962.

INDEX

Index

Persuasion in insurgency warfare, 66; *see also* Terror, terrorism

Philippines, 18, 54, 58, 64, 95, 100–1, 106–8, 149–50, 157; *see also* Hukbong Magpalaya Nang Bayan (People's Liberation Army) (HUK)

Phone Saly, 72; *see also* Laos

Photo reconnaissance, *see* Reconnaissance, aerial

Planning, 33, 47; *see also* Mao Tse-tung

"Politicization" of military forces, 37; *see also* Mao Tse-tung

Populace control
  in counterinsurgency warfare, 87–99, 116–7, 128, 136–54, 188
  in insurgency warfare, 66–8

Popular front organizations, *see* Front organizations

Propaganda
  in counterinsurgency warfare, 88–9
  in insurgency warfare, 30, 39, 40, 55, 59, 65, 66, 70–1, 73, 75
  see also Psychological warfare

Protracted conflict, 26, 30, 37

Pseudo-bands, 114; *see also* Small-scale operations

Psychological action, 117, 188
  definition of, 88

Psychological warfare
  in counterinsurgency warfare, 88–9, 104–9, 122–3, 170
  definition of, 88

in insurgency warfare, 20, 28, 55, 75, 106
  see also Propaganda

Public administration, *see* Civil administration in developing countries

Public works programs, 141–4; *see also* Military-civic action

Pye, Lucian, 144

Q

Quang Nagi, 125

R

Reconnaissance, aerial, 119–24

Recruitment
  in counterinsurgency warfare, 94
  in insurgency warfare, 40, 54–5, 65, 72–3, 185

Reform programs
  in counterinsurgency warfare, 83, 88–9, 92–9, 136, 138, 158, 161, 188–9 *passim*
  in insurgency warfare, 55–7
  see also Socioeconomic development

Regular armed forces
  in counterinsurgency warfare, 94, 107, 120, 131, 136–54, 157, 191
  in insurgency warfare, 73, 77, 185

Resettlement, 98, 100–3, 105, 117, 119–20, 125, 136, 188

"Revolutionary flow," 40, 59, 136, 189; *see also* Mao Tse-tung